Bin Laden, Islam, and America's New "War on Terrorism"

Bin Laden, Islam, and America's New "War on Terrorism"

As`ad AbuKhalil

AN OPEN MEDIA BOOK

SEVEN STORIES PRESS / NEW YORK

CONTENTS

ACKNOWLEDGMENTS

Greg Ruggiero of Seven Stories Press suggested that I write this book. I took the task with zeal at a time of great political stress in the wake of September 11 and its aftermath. I am grateful for the opportunity and for the editing and production process. I am also grateful to Yasmina Jraissati who worked on the editing of this book. I also wish to thank everybody who worked on this book at Seven Stories; those I know and those I do not yet know.

Maria R. Rosales, the most brilliant person I have yet encountered, has been the biggest influence in my life; both personally and intellectually. We remain close after our divorce. She alone knows of my gratitude and love. She read the entire manuscript, providing great editing and intellectual suggestions and insights. As always, Maria does things modestly.

I also wish to thank some of my friends with whom I have discussed the events covered in this book, specifically: Rhiannon Judd, Marina Throne-Holst, Bassam Haddad, Sinan Antun, Valerie Marleau, Tara Lynn Schendel, Zeina Zaatari, Bronwyn Leebaw, Julie Siebens, Ahmad Dallal, Shawna Bader, J.J. Hendricks, Rabi` `Aridi, Kathy Spillman, and `Imad al-Hajj. Samah Idriss so graciously opened the pages of *al-Adab* for my fulminations. Joseph Mas`ad, my close friend and intellectual interlocutor, has influenced my thinking on a number of issues, although I do not want to tell him that. Unfortunately, now he knows. My sister Mirvat has been extremely and generously supportive of my research and has consistently provided all sorts of help, although her last shipment of Arabic sweets was not spectacular. I am also grateful for her keen interest in my Arabic production.

My dear friend Luanne C. Peppers of Boston, MA, has provided so much help and so much friendship, despite the demands of her athletic career. She was especially helpful when I lost my internet connection for two long weeks. I have also discussed many of the issues and ideas covered here. Luanne also knows of my gratitude and friendship.

I also wish to thank J. J. Hendricks, the chairperson of my department, who has been extremely supportive during a very stressful semester, both as a chair and as a decent human being. Nezar AsSayyad, the chair of the Center for Middle Eastern Studies at the University of California, Berkeley, has also been supportive of my work. And for that I am grateful. I also wish to thank Larry Michalak of the same center for his years of support and interest.

I wish to express my gratitude to Sam Husseini, of Institute of Public Accuracy, who was insistent on disseminating my message throughout the media in the most intolerant of times. He, of course, should not be blamed for the hate mail that my media appearances generated. Also, I want to mention my students in California and Colorado for their unwavering support and friendship.

Finally, I dedicate this book to the memory of the innocent

As`ad AbuKhalil

victims of the terrorist bombings of September 11, and also to the memory of the innocent victims of U.S. bombing of Afghanistan. They all should have lived.

A NOTE ON TRANSLITERATION

In writing Arabic, I have diligently followed the old system of the Library of Congress (the one used by Hanna Batatu in his monumental *The Old Social Classes and the Revolutionary Movements of Iraq*).

However, for readability purposes, the transliteration had to be simplified: Diacritics could not be used, hence some different Arabic letters had to be romanized in the same way; diphthongs are not differentiated from vowels. Moreover, I chose to distinguish between the *shamsi* and the *qamari* letters—for example "al-Nabi" is spelled "an-Nabi"—for the English pronunciation to be as close as possible to the Arabic one.

At last, in order to avoid confusion, names and words that have entered the American vernacular are used here in the way they have been adopted through popular usage. For instance, "Qur'an" is more commonly spelled "Koran," "Usama bin Ladin" is spelled "Osama bin Laden," "Yasir `Arafat" is spelled "Yasser Arafat," and so forth.

This book was written with emotion, motivated by my anger at those who are willing to kill innocent people in New York City; Washington, DC; and Pennsylvania, followed by my anger at those who have been recklessly killing innocent people in Afghanistan and Palestine. I wrote this book for those without any background in Middle East studies or in Islam. It is partly for them, and partly for me. It is an attempt both to explain the background of the current crisis, and to express my feelings regarding the September 11 attacks and their aftermath.

This book deals with many issues and many regions of the world. It is essentially a primer for better understanding the current crisis. I have always mocked instant books, until I wrote one. I also must confess that I have been quite unhappy with the quality of books on the crisis and on bin Laden. Almost every single author of those books—with the exception of the fine journalist Ahmed Rashid—is a so-called terrorism expert or a journalist who cannot read Arabic or Persian, or any of the languages of spoken by the people of the Middle East or Asia. Of course, as some of the writers are former or current Israelis, they may know Hebrew. I wanted to utilize my close reading of non-English sources to share them with English readers around the world.

The style and tone of this book are emotional, and may

strike the academic reader as odd. But hiding behind the cloak of objectivity is often used more to conceal than to reveal. We are also not supposed to feel or to express anger, especially against the U.S. government, which academia often treats with more than a tinge of patriotism. As a citizen of both Lebanon and the United States, I suffer no pulls of patriotism toward either. This book was written from my deep belief in *human* identities and the deadly consequences of nationalism, although I agree with Sartre: "for the purpose of the Anti-Semite, I am a Jew." And living in the U.S. makes me say: for the purpose of the Anti-Arab, I am a proud Arab. I cannot, and could not, write about the events described with detachment and distance. I grew up in Lebanon and came to this country as a graduate student. I lived not far from Palestinian refugee camps. I have seen the devastation and human suffering caused by American weapons in Israeli hands, and also by U.S. forces in Lebanon in the 1980s. The events under study have shaped and molded me, for better or for worse. I lived through the civil war years of Lebanon, in which the U.S. was not a distant bystander. Since my childhood, the impact of Israeli occupation and brutality against the Arabs was a daily reality, not an abstract concept. Aside from the subjugation of the Palestinian people—which continues unabated, Israel has treated the people and region of South Lebanon (from which I hail) with condescension and contempt. I lived through the Israeli invasion of Lebanon in 1982, which resulted in the death of more than 15,000 Palestinian and Lebanese, mostly civilians. U.S. media barely, if ever, reported those deaths to Americans, while Israeli loss was mourned.

The story that is told is not a pleasant one. It entails murder, deception, duplicity, crude and subtle propaganda, war, defeat, racism, humiliation, oppression, misery, bigotry, and international domination and subjugation. It is, in many ways, the tale of the post-post Cold War, as Colin Powell has recently called it. It is the story of U.S. roles around the world, a story with which a majority of Americans are unfamiliar.

This book begins with an exposition of the impact and nature of Islamophobia in Western culture. I argue that we cannot dismiss the influence of Western fear and ignorance of Islam from current U.S. foreign policy making. The notion of a "clash of civilizations" is not new, I argue, and can be traced to the field of Western studies of Islam and the Middle East (what has historically been known by academics as Orientalism). The manifestations of anti-Islam and anti-Arab attitudes in the U.S. in particular, and less so in Europe, cannot but be related to the legacy of Islamophobia, the statements of U.S. officials (that "we are not against Islam") notwithstanding. Bombs dropped on Muslims speak louder than press releases and speeches.

I also offer remarks about the recent history of U.S. involvement in the Middle East. Americans often ask "why do they hate us?" but they never bother to find out. They seem content in accepting the assurances of leaders who suggest that "they hate us" because "they hate freedom," or because they hate "the American way of life," whatever that means. Looking at the history of U.S. relations in the region, I ask the reader to consider whether the impact of U.S. for-

As`ad AbuKhalil

eign policy is, in fact, the root cause of the mistrust and antipathy that are exhibited against the U.S. in the region. I also try to link U.S. roles in the Middle East with that in Afghanistan. One cannot understand the post-September 11 crisis in a vacuum.

In explaining the phenomenon of bin Laden and his fanatically violent movement, I include a brief review of contemporary Middle Eastern history, Islamic fundamentalism, and U.S. foreign policy toward the region. In doing so, I attempt to share with the reader a number of views and debates that often take place in Arabic and Persian, but not in English. As a Muslim-born secular Arab, I tried, not necessarily successfully, to read the literature of Islamic fundamentalism without subjecting it harshly to the scrutiny of secular humanism, with which I strongly identify.

Throughout, the book develops a critique of U.S. foreign policy that challenges the notion that U.S. actions are motivated by the longing to establish democracy and human rights for others. I offer an analogy between varieties of terrorism, like that of bin Laden and the violent actions of the United States. In so doing, it is my hope that by coming to terms with the suffering caused by U.S. influence and intervention abroad that the reader support the effort to call for a structurally and fundamentally different U.S. foreign policy—one which abides by international law, and holds the lives, rights, and diversities of other people and cultures as nothing less than equal to its own.

The attacks of September 11, 2001 have changed America forever, and will very clearly change the world. The event is ushering a new political era and new terminology. We already see old enemies being forgiven, and new ones entering the stage. Alliances are being formed and broken, and dissenters are under fire. As heroes are being declared and cheered, villains—preferably dark-skinned and turbaned—fill the TV screens. United, the government and people have focused on retaliation—not criminal investigation—in the form of open-ended war.

Far-reaching ideological and political shifts are under way. Suddenly, American liberals have accepted their conservative president, and act as if they have forgiven Republicans of their misdeeds. Even the champion of the 1960s students' anti-war movement, Todd Gitlin, is lashing out at those who he thinks are going too far in criticizing the United States.[1] Florida's election crisis is now an ancient memory. In the tragic aftermath of September 11, the president achieved unwavering support, and with it he lead the country to war. The mood is understandable, but is revenge the mark of a self-described "beacon of freedom," to use the language of George W. Bush? Is not the United States of America supposed to be the advanced civilization fighting against the inferior one, as the the Italian prime minister, Silvio Berlusconi, said?[2] Was this not what Samuel Huntington warned of in his now famous book, *The Clash of Civilization*,[3] in which he predicted the arrival of civilizational wars, with the Islamic world as a looming danger? With the country at war, little can occur to bring about a better understanding between the Middle East and the United States, no matter how many times the lone Arabic-speaking U.S. diplomat, Christopher Ross, appears on al-Jazeera TV.[4] The United States may be setting the stage for a confrontation that lasts for decades. This could be the war without end; a war the historians will say began on September 11. Middle East historians may trace it to earlier times, but despite the claims of many who insist that all Middle East animosities are to be traced back to the pre-Christian era, no one outside of religious circles actually does.[5]

In any case, the U.S. is at war, its troops are fighting on foreign soil, and as of January 2002, bin Laden and his entourage remain at large. Journalists reporting early "victories" appear giddy at Pentagon briefings and the nation feels proud of "the boys" in combat. Taliban control has been broken, and their bloody and oppressive record has been extensively covered. The president of the U.S. and his wife, oddly, sound like feminists when they chronicle the misogyny of the Taliban. But, though evidence of civilian casualties in Afghanistan fills the Arabic TV stations, they hardly appear on American TV. The new president of CNN, who in a previous role was largely responsible for the denigration of news and foreign affairs at *Time* magazine, warns, in a memo leaked to Howard Kurtz of the *Washington Post*, that too much coverage of Afghani civilian deaths may be inappropriate while our nation is at war.[6]

In short, although it has overpowered the Taliban and scattered al-Qaeda fighters in Afghanistan, the United States is far from achieving peace. The effect of the bombings, including the increase in the refugee population, worries humanitarian relief agencies. Conflict between regional "warlords," and the Northern Alliance and its enemies is not even close to being over. Old ethnic and tribal divisions in Afghanistan seem only to worsen with the advent of foreign troops and intervention. It is also highly unlikely that U.S. bombing will bring about an emancipation of Afghani women, not that this was ever a determinant of U.S. foreign policy. *Realpolitik* has no space for "soft" issues such as women's rights. In fact, before the World Trade Center tragedy, Bush seemed to anticipate that the Middle East would be pushed to the margins of U.S. foreign policy, despite the conditions women in Afghanistan faced. Unfortunately, September 11 brought the Middle East right back to the center of the *realpolitik* calculations of this administration.

Newly elected American presidents often assert their desire to steer away from the Middle East conflict. President George W. Bush was no exception. He was opposed to "nation building." He was determined to avoid getting bogged down in the Arab-Israeli conflict, preferring instead that the U.S. allow Israel to use its massive war machine to deal with the year-old Palestinian uprising. From the Israeli government's standpoint, his policy of "benign neglect" was

As`ad AbuKhalil

desirable because it gave Israel the advantage of tacit American support. Pro-Israeli pundits (like William Safire and Fouad Ajami[7]) have advocated it for decades.

The Arab regimes, on the other hand, always invite American intervention because they all are too aware of the volatility of the so-called Arab streets. Their fear of escalation leads Arab leaders to welcome American intercession on their behalf, despite the fact that hostility to American interests in the Middle East has characterized Arab popular culture since at least World War II. The reasons for this hostility are often shrouded in mystery; they sometimes are dismissed as the manifestation of fickle or mindless people.[8] Other times they are attributed to atavistic fervors of backward populations.[9]

Prejudiced images of Islam and Muslims derive from the long legacy of Western Orientalism (the classical field of teaching, writing, and knowing about things Islamic and Middle Eastern). Orientalism was the fountainhead of colonial knowledge of the Middle East, and it has long provided (im)moral and ideological justification for the subjugation of the peoples of the region. America's "new war on terrorism" has revived the desire to explain away the beliefs of Muslims and Arabs, although now the explanations are more likely to revolve around the irrational fear of freedom and democracy that such people supposedly share.

1

ISLAMOPHOBIA

I n the modern age, it may be hazardous to speak about a "West" or about an "Islam." Though neither the West nor Islam exist as monolithic entities, journalists and politicians insist on framing the current situation in these terms. It was Huntington who most recently popularized the framework of the clash of civilizations, but the concept was introduced long before him by Princeton historian Bernard Lewis. As evidence that this framework is operational again, consider the fact that Lewis was recently brought back from retirement to serve as a consultant on the Middle East for the U.S. government,[10] and in November 2001 he was awarded a seat on NBC's widely watched *Meet the Press*. He has even been to the White House during the crisis but remains coy on whether he had a *tête-à-tête* with the president. Such is his influence in today's America. Lewis has been urging the government to deal toughly with Muslims and Arabs, and wants the U.S. to project its power on them.[11] For Bernard Lewis, there is an advanced, humane West, and then there is "Islam," which includes religion, law, civilization, geography, and history. In his mind, Muslims and Islam have not changed over the centuries; for him, studying a 9th century Arabic manuscript is useful methodologically to explain the political behavior of Palestinians in 2002. In his book *Islam and the West,*[12] which no student of Middle Eastern politics can escape, he elaborates on such concepts and treats all Muslims as one homogeneous group. According to him, all Muslims have similar characteristics and modes of behavior, and their nasty deeds can all be explained by reference to the Koran and classical books of jurisprudence, with which he is quite familiar. In his brilliant book *La fascination de l'Islam,* French Orientalist Maxime Rodinson examines the concept of theologocentrism—the attribution of all observable phenomena among Muslims to matters of Islamic theology.[13] Rodinson was disturbed by the persistence of this school, and by its influence, which extends far beyond the realm of academia. During the Gulf War, for example, and again during the current crisis, the Koran becomes a best selling book. During the opening weeks of the "new war on terrorism," British Prime Minister Tony Blair was reported to be studying the Koran.[14] How nice, but why? People rush to study Islam as if it offers *the* skeleton key to understanding the political complexities of the Middle East. Unfortunately, it seems as if only when Muslims are accused of terrorism that the impulse arises to educate the public about Islam, thereby creating—wittingly or unwittingly—an irrevocable association between Islam and terrorism. Of course, it is hard for many to accept that Islam may not be the most useful paradigm to explain the behavior of people who happen to be Muslims, or that Muslims, like other people of the world, are also driven by socio-economic, political, and cultural forces. When it is useful, however, the U.S. government leaves its theologocentrism aside. During the Cold War most aberrant political behavior of Muslims was attributed not to Islam, but to communism.

Though theologocentrism is inane, Islam is without argument a force throughout many Middle East countries. Saudi Arabia has emblazoned on its flag the *shahadah*, one of the five pillars of Islam which proclaims "I attest that there is no Allah but Allah, and that Muhammad is the Messenger of Allah." Both Arab leaders and their opponents regularly invoke religious language in their speeches. Whether their deference is sincere or not, this dictates a certain lingo in Islamic political cultures and it establishes real social parameters in many regions, parameters which the faithful many believe to have been ordered by God.

Nevertheless, in the West, particularly in the United States, the political exploitation of religion goes on unabated. When Governor George W. Bush was running for president, for example, he asserted that Jesus was his favorite political philosopher; and as president, he now begins all his cabinet meetings with a prayer.[15] During President Bill Clinton's impeachment crisis he was seen every Sunday leaving church with his personal copy of the Bible in hand. Despite the separation of church and state, religious image is part of a politician's public persona used to build—and influence—its constituent base. Reverend Billy Graham has served a useful purpose for presidents since the days of Harry Truman (although Harry Truman later banned Graham from the White House for telling the press details of his private prayer session with the president). Every war that this country enters seems to require his blessing, and fortunately for presidents, Rev. Graham has not met a war that he did not find just. The Syrian intellectual Sadiq Jalal al-`Adhm refers to Graham as "Ayatollah Billy Graham." Graham's son and successor, Franklin, recently expressed his views on Islam, declaring that it is an "evil" religion, one that must be fought.

Likewise, the political language of Arab governments (there is no such thing as the political language of Islam, as a title of a book by Bernard Lewis insists[16]), is filled with koranic quotations and *Hadith* citations. These governments, all of which are completely lacking democratic legitimacy, are in a constant campaign to demonstrate their piety, and thus legitimacy. Just as the political demands on Bush and Clinton lead them to parade their piety, make public blessings, and invoke God, the calculations on the part of Arab government leaders dictate that they make a strong expressions of faith and claim that they march on the path of the Prophet, or *sunnah*, in Arabic.

The assertion by Arab leaders that they are simply following the will of God is one which also permeates political culture in Western societies. Westerners are inclined to believe that Islam guides the behavior of all Middle Easterners. This explains why media outlets rushed to interview Islamic experts after the World Trade Center bombing in 1993, and rushed to print "educational" articles on Islam in the wake of the September 11 attacks. Even when the U.S. government makes public efforts to absolve Islam, it accepts the political salience of Islam in the political debate over ter-

rorism. For example, when Colin Powell gave an unprecedented interview to the Arabic daily *al-Hayat* on September
26, 2001, he excoriated Muslims to free their religion from
the influence of terrorists. Yet one does not hear any appeals
to the Pope or to Protestant ministers to free their religion
from the stranglehold of terrorists when anti-abortion clinics are bombed or when Christian criminals carry out violent acts. This pattern illustrates theologocentrism born of
Islamophobia, and of course, it has a history to it.

It used to be that the West (as it is collectively known)
had dealt with Islam only as a threat; first in the form of a
rapidly expanding empire in the seventh century, and later
in the form of unruly countries that had to be colonized
after World War II. In its dealings with Muslim and Arab
countries today, the West has not left behind this past of
"civilizational conflict" as the Italian Prime Minister's
comments recently demonstrated. This, ironically, is not
lost on Islamic fundamentalists, who also approach their
enmity to the West as a civilizational struggle; for them
there is an all-encompassing West as there is an all-encompassing Islam. From this view has emerged the methodolo-
gy of the Muslim Brothers,[17] the precursors of modern
Islamic fundamentalism, since at least the 1960s, when
famed Egyptian writer Muhammad al-Ghazzali wrote his
book on *al-Ghazw al-Fikri* (cultural invasion), in reference
to Western influences in Muslim societies. As the West was
increasingly asserting its influence, the advocates of
Muslim authenticity often dubbed the *salafiyyah* movement (literally, those who wish to return to the predeces-

As`ad AbuKhalil

sor's purity and benevolence) raised alarm over the erosion of Islamic values and mores.

Thus, theologocentrism also exists among Muslims. But among many non-Muslims it has been transformed into an ideology of hostility, which is comparable in its features to traditional racism, like anti-Semitism. Thus, to theologo-centrists, all Muslims form one monolithic block, and they all possess the same characteristics and exhibit the same modes of behavior and conduct. To validate this view, there is always an effort to collect documentation that would prove one's views to others, for example, that evil is real, and that an entire group is possessed by it, both individually and as a block. Israeli embassies around the world are more than willing to provide "useful" translations of Arabic articles from obscure journals and books to prove the evil intentions of Arabs and Muslims. Listening to foreign policy hearings in the U.S. Congress, one would think that most Senate and House members are fluent in Arabic, as many of them cite various Arabic sources in their diatribes against the Palestinians and other Arabs. Furthermore, many still cite classical Orientalists, who were willing to draw upon ancient Islamic jurisprudence to falsely claim that Muslims can only recognize two spheres in international relations: the abode of Muslims and the abode of infidels. Historically, the Prophet and Islamic laws were more flexible and prag-matic. For example, Muhammad signed peace treaties with Christians and with pagans. The notion that Muslims can-not coexist with non-Muslims for theological reasons, as is being asserted as of late, is utterly false. No contemporary

Muslim theologians question the faithfulness of the millions of Muslims who live in religiously mixed societies.

Anti-Arab and anti-Muslim ideologies have served a very useful purpose. By attributing all manifestations of Arab and Muslim political behavior to religion, authentic political grievances are easily avoided. Thus, from a theologocentric view, Palestinian political opposition to Israel is neatly attributed to religious anti-Semitism. While it is possible to locate anti-Jewish passages in the Koran and other authoritative Islamic sources, it is not easy to reconcile classical anti-Semitism with Islamic theology. Islamic theology accepts, on principle, the partnership between Jews, Muslims, and Christians in the worship of the same God. There certainly is nothing comparable to Christian anti-Semitism in the Islamic heritage, and in reading modern anti-Semitic writings by some Islamic fundamentalists one often finds references to the diaries of Henry Ford and other Western anti-Semitic works.

The image of the "Islamic" terrorist allows xenophobia against Arabs and Muslims to intensify. And, not unlike medieval forms of prejudice, it takes the deed of only one member of a group to taint and stigmatize the whole group. A clear example of this was how the U.S. media used Sirhan Sirhan, the assassin of Robert Kennedy in 1968, to characterize the entire community of Palestinians as terrorists. In other words, as in classical forms of prejudice, diversity is not perceived to exist within a stigmatized group. There is only "typical" and "representative" behavior. All members of the group are believed to adhere to the same standards and to the same modes of behavior. And post-September 11 references to "sleeper cells" of terrorists "in our midst" exacerbate Islamophobia and suggest that American Muslims and Arabs may commit terrorist acts at the drop of a hat. While the origins of contemporary attitudes toward Muslims and Arabs can be traced back to Latin polemics against Islam and Saracens,[18] the influential pro-Israeli lobby in the U.S. has spent millions to mobilize the population behind the Israeli stance in the Arab-Israeli conflict. Israel was, and is, seen as a part of Western civilization engaged in a fight against forces that are not also members. Zionist leaders, including T. Herzl and Chaim Weizman, were not timid in expressing their positions in strikingly civilizational terms. Herzl promised to bring European civilization to the Holy Land, and his European interlocutors were pleased.

It is remarkable that the ideological roots of the Crusades have been preserved almost intact up through modern times. Arabs are stereotyped as cruel, duplicitous, savage, backward, uncouth, and civilizationally inept. The behavior of Arab leaders, which is in no way different from the behavior of other political leaders worldwide, is often explained with references to peculiar Arab traits, or to the "temperament" or "mind" of the Arabs, to cite the titles of two books that aim to demystify the enigma of Arab personal and political behavior.[19] A different treatment of these issues can be found in the last chapter of Edward Said's influential book, *Orientalism*.

Manifestations of Islamophobia have intensified since September 11. The nationwide—and largely arbitrary—arrests of Arabs only attest to the persistent suspicion toward all

Arabs and all Muslims. While hundreds of Arabs have been arrested, not a single one of them, by the admission of the Justice Department, has had, as of early 2002, any tie to either bin Laden or the hijackers. Only one has been indicted on purely circumstantial evidence. Moreover, civil libertarians have raised questions about the method of assembling the list of hijackers' names, apparently based only on their ethnicity. Muslim and Arab-American organizations compound the problem by continuously issuing condemnations of all terrorist attacks, thereby putting themselves and their faith on the defensive, as if their citizenship is conditional on certain political declarations, and as if the obvious abhorrence of violence is a non-Muslim, non-Arab trait. In comparison, Irish-Americans are never asked nor expected to condemn IRA terrorism. In the myopic tradition of McCarthyism, "experts" interviewed by media—most of whom have no command of any of the languages spoken by the Muslims of Asia—assert the culpability of Muslim organizations, and Daniel Pipes,[20] Steven Emerson,[21] Fouad Ajami,[22] and Mamoun Fandy[23] among others, sound as if all those who criticize U.S. government can be somehow linked to terrorism.

In the world portrayed by U.S. media, there has developed an organic link between Islam and violence. The violence of Muslims is terrorism, while Western violence is reported and understood by a different set of standards and a different set of terms. This tendency is combined with the theologo-centric belief that violent acts committed by Muslims are "Islamic" violence, while violence of Western groups is rarely, if ever, portrayed in religious terms. Explaining

As`ad AbuKhalil

abhorred behavior in solely religious, ethnic, or racial terms fuels hate crimes and the irrationality that gives rise to violence like that of the Ku Klux Klan, Nazis, or the Jewish Defense League, with leaders of the latter group having been recently indicted on charges of plotting to bomb a mosque and the office of an Arab-American congressperson.[24]

Unfortunately, Islamic fundamentalists, for purposes of grassroots legitimization and mobilization, often characterize their acts in terms that add fuel to the fire. Declaring war against "Jews and Crusaders," as bin Laden has done, and explaining away bombings and hijackings as *jihad*—a term used in the Koran—further exacerbate Western Islamophobia, racial profiling, and polarization. But when Christian fanatics like David Koresh or Rev. Sun Myung Moon claim to be Jesus Christ, they are not taken all that seriously, while the religious fulminations of Islamic fanatics are translated, studied, and taken as representative opinion.

In turn, Arabic words like *jihad* come to be used for sensational impact in Western media, and are grossly misunderstood. Etymologically, the word refers to struggle in general, or striving for whatever purpose. More importantly, the Koran in no way uses the concept to exclusively refer to holy war.

In Chapter `Ankabut (29:8) of the Koran, for example, the verb *jahada* is used to connote "trying hard; and in Surat at-Tawbah (24:9), it talks about a general unspecified *jihad* for "the sake of God." In fact, it is clear in the koranic context that God accepts a variety of forms of *jihad* (or struggle), and refers to "those who migrated and practiced the *jihad* of money and spirit," in verse 73 of Surat al-Anfal (Chapter the Spoils). Yet, militant fundamentalist and militant Western anti-Arabs often find it convenient to quote the same chapter but from verse 61, which says: "muster against them whatever force you can...horrifying"—not *terrorizing* as translators often have it—"the enemy of God and your enemy..." But it is made clear in the context of the Koran that God is referring not to all unbelievers, but to those among them who break contracts and violate treaties.

The Koran clearly states that starting wars is immoral. In fact, a few verses later, in verse 62, it adds: "and if they tilt toward peace, tilt toward it."[25] It is precisely this verse which Anwar Sadat invoked in order to rationalize his peace initiative toward Israel.

In the *Hadith*—the body of sayings and deeds attributed to the Prophet Muhammad, which is second only to the direct word of God in the Koran—*jihad* has two meanings. *Greater Jihad* refers to a person's internal spiritual struggle to become a better human being. *Smaller Jihad* refers to acts of combat for purposes of defending one's community and faith. And one particular *Hadith* (reported in the "reliable" *Sahih* collection[26]) states that a Muslim who went to a prophet to inform him of his intention to perform battle for Islam, was told that he should perform "*jihad* for his parents," meaning that his care for his old parents is real *jihad*. And a forthcoming book by the late chairperson of the Islamic Shi`ite Supreme Council in Lebanon, Muhammad Mahdi Shams ad-Din, whose influence and judgment extended far beyond Lebanon and far beyond Shi`ism, illus-

trates that Muslim jurists have in fact very tightly restrict-
ed the application of the military *jihad*, and that fighting
infidels was not a casual affair to be taken on by any
Muslim.[27] Shams ad-Din maintains that a consensus exist-
ed among Muslim jurisprudents throughout history that
military *jihad* could only be launched against "those infidels who are not linked with Muslims through treaties or
through truces."[28] Even the prophet signed and adhered to
treaties with pagans, though pagans are the least tolerated in
Islam, while Jews and Christians are theologically accepted
as worshippers of the same God.

Of course, Islam, like Judaism and Christianity, is not a
pacifist religion, but to view it as an exclusively violent religion is the product of historical prejudice and ignorance. To
be sure, there exist Muslim clerics who use their freedom to
interpret religious texts—there is no central papal authority
in Islam—in order to advocate violence as an expedient for
social and political change. It is not theology that drives
these clerics, but politics and economics. The climate in
which the (mis)use of religion takes place is purely political.
For example, the struggle against the Egyptian government
by Muslim fundamentalists in the 1980s and 1990s was
inspired by opposition to the policies and actions of the government, and not by passages of the Koran. Despite this, the
concept of *jihad*, and all complex social, cultural, and economic nuances that drive politics are flattened out and lost
in the media, and never more crudely so since the media's
post-September 11 adoption of George Bush's polarized
"with us or against us" language of "good" vs. "evil."

Some may point to the statements made by the Bush administration that attempt to distinguish between "good Muslims" and "bad Muslims." Yet when the secretary of state calls on Muslims to speak out against "bad Muslims," he implies that there is a problem within the religion itself. The secretary's call may seem appropriate and unbiased in the wake of the September 11 attacks. But the real profound biases of the culture are revealed in the simple fact that the same logic is not applied to all: Christian leaders are not exhorted to reign in "bad Christians" after abortion clinics are bombed by Christian fundamentalists or when African-Americans and immigrants are victimized by the burning crosses and hate crimes of the KKK. The culture's blind spot toward its own prejudice is revealed by the fact that KKK bombings and killings are not described as terrorism. Similarly, Israeli terrorists living among settlers operate freely with the support of the government of Israel in the occupied territories of the West Bank and Gaza, are not described as terrorists, and no one calls to reform Judaism or calls for a war "within Judaism" the way that Thomas Friedman of the *New York Times* calls for a war "within Islam."[29] And after the assassination of Israeli prime minister Rabin by a Jewish theology student, no calls were issued by the U.S. or Israeli media to reform the teachings of Jewish religious schools.

In reality, the fundamentalists of the three faiths are quite similar in outlook and objective: they all are intolerant, misogynist, obscurantist, homophobic, puritanical, armed, and willing to use violence to advance their causes.

2

PRE-SEPTEMBER 11 U.S. POLICY TOWARD
THE MIDDLE EAST AND "ISLAM"

U.S. relations with the Middle East and with "Islam" (meaning with Muslim people and organizations worldwide) have been deteriorating over for years. The rise of Islamic fundamentalists in most Muslim countries has meant that oppressive U.S. policies (and U.S. society) are more harshly judged. The rise of the religious right in the U.S. and the arrival of the Clinton administration solidified U.S. ties with Israel, which had always been close. Under Clinton, the alliance between the two states grew closer; intelligence ties increased, and all but one of Israel's previous demands—the release of convicted Israeli spy, Jonathan Pollard—were met. In fact, President Clinton intended to release Pollard, but yielded when CIA director George Tenet reportedly threatened to resign over the matter. Even the sharing of raw data from U.S. intelligence satellites, which even Reagan prohibited, was permitted by the Clinton administration. U.S. relations with Israel are but one of many aspects of U.S. foreign policy that are a major source of irritation and resentment in the Middle East, especially in Muslim countries.

U.S. foreign policy in the Middle East has been sordid. After the violent establishment of Israel in 1948, the U.S. committed itself increasingly to the side of the new nation. The decision to recognize the state of Israel was not an easy one; several personalities and institutions within the U.S. government opposed the recognition of Israel, warning of its deadly consequences for American interests in the Middle East and beyond. Despite the opposition of Secretary of Defense James Forrestal and most of the foreign policy experts,[30] President Truman forged forward and established U.S. support for Israel.

The basis for U.S.-Israeli relations can be traced back to the Holocaust and official inaction that the U.S. government for too long exhibited toward the Nazi's massacre of Jews. Furthermore, the U.S., up until 1944, was restrictive of Jewish refugees who sought shelter in the U.S. For the British and American governments, it was easier to support unlimited Jewish immigration when the refugees were moving to someone else's territory; the Holy Land. U.S.-Israeli relations continued to grow and develop during the Cold War when Israel served as a bulwark against Soviet expansion in the Middle East, and its military and intelligence were used to smash and fight liberation movements and progressive organizations, from Oman to the Western Sahara. The rise of pro-Soviet governments in Syria, Egypt, and Iraq at different times in the 1950s and 1960s, allowed Israel to align its wars against Arab states with America's Cold War strategies against the Soviets. Yet, for U.S. liberals and leftists, Israel was seen as a progressive socialist experiment that inspired support. Over the years, Israelis have managed to successfully market themselves to both the left and the right.

In 1956, U.S.-Israeli relations suffered their most serious crisis when President Eisenhower forced Israel to withdraw

As`ad AbuKhalil

from occupied Egyptian territories. France, Britain, and Israel had launched a tripartite invasion of Egypt in the hope of toppling popular Egyptian leader Jamal Abdul-Nasser, who dared to nationalize the Suez Canal in the same year. [31] Instead of toppling him, the crisis propelled him into the position of the undisputed pan-Arab leader who defied three external powers. Nasser wanted to establish good ties with the United States, but American refusal to sell him weapons, and heavy-handed American treatment of his government, forced him to direct himself increasingly toward Moscow, while continuing to oppress Egyptian communists. Despite tension between Egypt and America, the Eisenhower administration apparently thought that it was too much to accept Israeli troops remaining in Egypt. The U.S. was also envious of British influence in the Middle East; influence that it was trying to displace.

A few years later, John F. Kennedy tried to address the issue of Palestinian refugees. He even talked about applying UN resolutions pertaining to Israeli (mis)treatment of Palestinians. Strong voices within the Democratic Party prevailed, and Kennedy soon disregarded the Middle East crisis altogether.[32] Many supporters of Israel saw this "benign neglect" as a step forward.

Lyndon Johnson took U.S. foreign policy with Israel to another level; he viewed the Arab-Israeli relations in terms similar to his view of the Texas vs. Mexico conflict.[33] He wanted Israel to prevail in the June 1967 war, and he all but gave the green light for Israel to attack Syria and Egypt combined.

Nixon solidified U.S.-Israeli relations further. In order to save Israel in the 1973 war, he authorized the most massive airlift of arms ever conducted. As intended, the airlift managed to turn the war in Israel's favor.[34]

Successive U.S. presidents continued the trend of increasing support for Israel. Ronald Reagan set the grounds for future presidents by treating Israel as a special non-NATO ally and friend. Even though Israel's per capita income is comparable to that of many European countries, Israel became the largest recipient of U.S. aid. Today Israel receives more aid than the entire sub-Saharan African region. U.S. policies under Reagan established that the American government would support an Israeli military edge over neighboring Arab governments, a policy which continues to this day.

Though ties with Israel are a defining element of U.S. foreign policy in the Middle East, the U.S. has many other key—albeit less central—regional connections. Turkey—or the military generals of Turkey who maintain the behind the scenes power—have also served as a key element in U.S. Middle East policy. Turkey's membership in NATO has given its military leadership an edge over its non-NATO neighbors. Turkey has utilized this advantage in its internal oppression of all of forms dissent, especially the persecution of Kurds, and the intimidation of its neighbors during the Cold War. Turkey has killed as many Kurds as has Saddam Hussein's regime in Iraq, if not more. This powerful Muslim country has served U.S. regional interests, and the strong regime does not hesitate to identify with U.S. foreign policy

As`ad AbuKhalil

goals, unlike the timid Saudi royal family that always looks over its shoulders in constant fear of dissent and conspiracy.

Oil is another powerful consideration shaping U.S. foreign policy, particularly in the Middle East. This consideration has elevated America's "friendship" with Saudi Arabia—whose royal family established the kingdom in the 1930s after striking an alliance with the Sunni Wahhabi clerical establishment. The strategic security of "moderate Arab regimes" involves a relation with the U.S. in which the U.S. offers weapon systems and protection—as was the case with Kuwait during the Gulf War—in return for political and economic subservience. Indeed, Saudi Arabia has strived to uphold U.S. economic interests by playing an instrumental role within the Organization of the Petroleum Exporting Countries (OPEC)—the organization that includes most oil producing countries with the exception of the U.S., Russia, and UK—in order to increase production whenever oil prices increase to a level that threatens the stability of prices in Western economies. This relationship, however, has not been without tensions and conflict. In 1973, in response to overt U.S. military support for Israel during the Arab-Israeli war, Saudi Arabia briefly, and very symbolically, stopped exporting oil to the U.S., which was partly responsible for triggering an oil crisis.[35]

Though all these were important factors in U.S. relations with the Middle East, U.S. policy was perhaps most driven by its Cold War strategy. So intent was the U.S. in neutralizing communist influences and conspiracies, that it sometimes found them even when they did not exist. For example, former CIA Near East expert Archie Roosevelt lamented that the U.S. unwisely equated manifestations of Arab nationalism with Soviet communism, thereby unwittingly alienating potential Arab allies of the United States.[36] But the U.S. would have been unable to win Arab popular support anyway, as long as it insisted on identifying so strongly with Israeli militancy.

Furthermore, it is important to realize that the Oslo process, which was hailed as a victory by the U.S., was met with skepticism and hostility in much of the Middle East. Arabs did not trust Israel's Oslo Accord signatory, Rabin. They viewed him not as a peacemaker, but as a war criminal for his role in the physical eviction of Palestinians from their homes in 1948, and for his brutal policies during his years as chief of staff, defense minister, and later prime minister. Additionally, the Israelis went to Oslo with a good deal of apprehension, and successive Israeli leaders from the Rightist Likud to the Centrist Labor made it very clear that the Israeli government was going to pick and chose what to implement from Oslo, and according to a timetable of its own choosing. Arab public opinion, and even some Arab governments, considered the Oslo deal unfair to the Palestinians and faulted Yasser Arafat for squandering decades of Palestinian struggle to save his own political career, which barely withstood the consequences of the Gulf War.

The Oslo process ostensibly sought to achieve a genuine resolution to the Arab-Israeli conflict: official Palestinian recognition of Israeli statehood and security (the Palestinians are never seen as deserving of security) in return for Israeli withdrawal from some Palestinian lands occupied in 1967. The rest was left for Israel to define and identify.

Previous attempts to install the Jordanian monarch, King Hussein, as representative of the Palestinians, reached a dead end in the 1980s. These attempts had been made repeatedly despite the Palestinian people's near unanimous contempt for him and his family for their double-dealings with the Zionists, and for their war against the Palestinians in 1970-71, known as Black September.

The Oslo agreements brought about a division of Palestinian lands into three zones: one ostensibly under "full" Palestinian control; another under joint Israeli-Palestinian control; and a third under full Israeli control. But the process did not force Israel to stop building settlements in Palestinian territories, and Israel maintained control of the land, water, and space even of territories ostensibly held by Palestinians. All the thorny issues, like the plight of millions of Palestinian refugees, the presence of armed Jewish settlers in Palestinian lands, the status of Jerusalem, and the delineation of borders were left unmentioned or postponed until future negotiations.[37]

What became quickly clear to the Arab world was that American leadership would never punish the Israelis for violating the Oslo accords or for its continued violent oppression of Palestinians. It also became clear to many Arabs that the Palestinians were the only party expected to adhere strictly to the terms of the agreement. The Oslo accords have built-in mechanisms to punish Palestinian infractions, but no similar mechanisms to punish Israeli violations. The U.S. government simply would not or could not pressure Israel to the extent needed to achieve an agreement that was genuinely balanced and fair. Thus, Oslo by definition was fundamentally imbalanced and unfair, reflecting a regional and international political climate fiercely unfavorable to the Palestinians.

Regarding the subsequent U.S.-brokered Camp David summit of 2000, the prevalent view that the Palestinians had wasted a great opportunity in the face of unprecedented Israeli offers was later contradicted by official sources, including one of President Clinton's advisors on Palestinian affairs.[38] We now learn that Israel not only did not offer as much land as was maintained, but effectively divided the West Bank into three cantons, which were barely connected and under tight Israeli control, and that the rights of the refugees were largely disregarded. In reality, the Palestinian uprising, covered extensively throughout the Arab world, had been going on unabated since September 2000. Ongoing Israeli oppression of Palestinians and the reckless violations of agreements that the Israeli government had signed only proved to Arab public opinion that Israel was not serious about reaching a peaceful accommodation with the Palestinians. It also caused the Arab public to believe that the U.S. government would never punish Israel for its actions, regardless of how far Israel went in its violent campaigns against a largely defenseless population, and regardless of how outraged international public opinion became. In this respect, the U.S. was virtually alone in its endorsement of Israeli violence.

The emergence of George W. Bush has only raised the ire

As`ad AbuKhalil

of most Arabs. Bush's ignorance of foreign and domestic policy was legendary, and his statements on the Arab-Israeli conflict were damaging and provocative. When he traveled to
Israel as a presidential candidate, he showered praise on Ariel
Sharon and hailed him as a hero. Bush may not have known
that his own father, during his administration, banned U.S.
government contact with Sharon for his opposition to the
"peace process." Bush also may not have heard of Lebanon's
Sabra and Shatila massacres, for which Sharon is held responsible even by an Israeli commission of inquiry (though "indirectly" responsible is the official language of the commission). His foreign policy team, which would play a very
important role given his limited knowledge of world affairs,
was solidly pro-Israeli. Bush's image worsened after his election. As Israeli/Palestinian violence continued to escalate—
with a ratio in 2001 of approximately one Israeli for every six
Palestinians killed—Bush's anger at the Palestinians seemed
to increase. As the Palestinian death toll rose, his demands for
a Palestinian "end to terrorism" increased with it. He has
refused to meet Arafat in the White House. The administration's team, especially in the Department of Defense, the
National Security Council, and the Office of the Vice
President, have all been solidly pro-Likud. Only Secretary of
State Colin Powell and his loyal deputy represent a relative
alternative. Yet, when Israel demolished more than 50 houses
of Palestinians in January 2002, forcing its hundreds of inhab-
itants to live under the skies amid a cruel snow storm, Colin
Powell justified Israeli actions as "self-defense." Such is the
world of U.S. foreign policy making toward the Middle East.

The significance of the Arab-Israeli conflict to U.S. policy toward the Middle East and Islam has been belittled by the powerful pro-Israel lobby. The lobby often argues that there are no repercussions to U.S. support for Israel, and that many Middle East sources exaggerate the extent of Arab public support for the plight of Palestinians. To the contrary, public opinion surveys in the Arab world all indicate that the Palestinian question remains a "core issue," as Michael Hudson calls it, and that it symbolically reflects the wrongs of American foreign policy. In 2001, Arab public reactions to Israeli oppression of Palestinians have been unprecedented, although the U.S. media have largely ignored them. Demonstrations in places like Qatar, Oman, Saudi Arabia, and the United Arab Emirates protesting Israeli violence against Palestinians indicated that Arab popular anger was capable of affecting the stability of many Arab regimes. It was in response to such expressions of outrage that the Arab summit was held early in 2001. This summit did not deliver solutions; they never do. But the meeting itself, which is always dreaded by many Arab leaders who do not get along and prefer to avoid one another, is a measure of the different regimes' concern over public opinion in their home countries.

For Arabs, the plight of the Palestinians is both a humanitarian and symbolic issue. It is a humanitarian problem that most Arabs know all too well; they have all dealt with Palestinians and have read Arabic literature that is full of references to the plight of the dispossessed population. Symbolically, it exposes the weaknesses and impotence of Arab governments vis-à-vis Israel, as it exposes the deep

As`ad AbuKhalil

American commitment to Israeli militancy. The miserable conditions in which most Palestinians live represent the injustices that the Arabs feel the West has inflicted on the Arab and Muslim peoples, particularly the West's historical refusal to acknowledge the true roots and scope of Palestinian suffering. It took more than 50 years since the establishment of Israel for a U.S. president to utter the word "Palestine," and he—George W. Bush—uttered the unspeakable word in response to strong Saudi pressure following the attacks of September 11.

With respect to oil, the U.S. plays a heavy-handed role, wanting oil producers in the Middle East to second their own interests in order to prioritize American corporations and consumers. American politicians fear a backlash from the electorate over pump prices. In the last few years, the U.S. has sent its secretary of energy to pressure Saudi Arabia to increase production as much as U.S. energy needs require, and to cajole other OPEC members into following the Saudi track. The U.S. would often urge Saudi Arabia to call for a special OPEC meeting just to accommodate American demands and needs. This, of course, does not go over well in the Middle East. The popular Egyptian leader Jamal Abdul-Nasser raised the slogan: "Arab oil is for the Arabs" in the face of Western economic and political domination. Blatant American intervention in oil production and pricing strikes many Arabs as an assault on regional sovereignty, and as a reflection of Western hegemony. The priority of domestic economic concerns has lifted the veil of quiet diplomacy from U.S. energy policy. Similar to its policy on global warming, the U.S. places high profit and low prices above all else, no matter what consequences it may have for the rest of the planet.

In addition to Israeli militancy and U.S. oil policy, a third issue of potent emotional intensity to Arabs are the U.S.'s ongoing sanctions against Iraq. While U.S. media rarely cover the impact of the sanctions or the implications of the 10-plus years of almost weekly bombing of Iraqi targets, the Arab press is saturated with daily and regular coverage of the continuing suffering of the Iraqi people. The U.S. government is clearly unaware of the depth of Arab feelings on the issue.[39] Again, only Colin Powell appears to acknowledge the significance of the issue. He promised to review of the sanctions—"smart sanctions" is what he called them— as soon as he assumed the office of secretary of state. He subsequently proposed a new set of sanctions that would ostensibly alleviate the suffering of the civilian population, a proposal which was immediately disapproved by both the White House and Capitol Hill. Instead of attempting to mitigate the impact of the sanctions on civilians, Bush has been pushing for an increase in the sanctions' severity. In the Arab world, the torment of the Iraqi people has been added to the A-list of grievances against the U.S. government, and may be a key reason why some in the Middle East gloated over the New York tragedy. Accounts of civilian deaths appear daily the Arab press, and many lament Western indifference.

Similarly, the plight of Afghanistan had been receding from American radar screens for years prior to September 11;

As`ad AbuKhalil

the stories of civil war there were rarely reported, and the conflict between the Taliban and the Northern Alliances were covered—when covered—though a "they-have-been-killing-each-others-for-ages" line, thereby absolving U.S. of any responsibility in the carnage. In the Middle East, the tale of Afghanistan is vividly remembered, and that the U.S. supplied all factions, especially the most religiously fanatic among them, with weapons, training, and ammunition, provided that they hated communism. Nor has it been forgotten that the U.S. helped to catalyze the creation of an international fundamentalist network, the very same that it now wants to eradicate. But the tale of U.S. support for Islamic fundamentalism goes even farther back into history, and will be covered later.

Arab and Middle Eastern opposition to U.S. foreign policy also includes the historical support that the American government has given to most of the oppressive regimes of the region. While the United States propagates news of human rights violations of its enemies—like Libya and Iran—severe human rights violations conducted by regional allies like Saudi Arabia, where political and religious oppression is perhaps worse than any other country in the Middle East, do not get any attention in the U.S. media. You do not hear the Feminist Majority (which supported a war against Afghanistan in the name of helping Afghani women) organizing a campaign against the Saudi Royal family. Barbara Boxer, an ostensible champion of women's rights worldwide, does not raise her voice in opposition to Saudi oppression, perhaps because Saudi arms purchases help California's economy. Saudi Arabia's role in smashing opposition movements in the region, and in sponsoring reactionary religious organizations, is noted by Arabs, but is rarely reported Western countries.

3

AFGHANISTAN IN THE WAKE
OF THE COLD WAR

Afghanistan's location has greatly shaped its history and the makeup of its population. The country has been sandwiched between the great powers of India, Persia, Russia, and Uzbekistan. Its rugged terrain and harsh ecology gave it an aura of invincibility, although invaders never stopped trying to control it. Islam arrived there as early as the seventh century. Early Arab chroniclers took note of the distinction of the local cultures and peoples. Traveling through what is today Afghanistan, the great Arab traveler Ibn Battutah observed in the 14th century: "Kabul, which in the past used to be a great city, is now a village inhabited by Persian speakers called Afghans. They have mountains and passage ways, and they have a strong resolve. Most of them are bandits."[40] Contrary to the claims of V. S. Naipaul that Islam smashes local cultures and flavors, Arabic Islam mostly allowed local cultures to exist and sometimes to flourish. Without this flexibility Islam could not have expanded beyond Mecca and Medina and spread throughout the world.

But Afghanistan cannot be described as a separate entity with cultures distinct from the surroundings. The names of the ethnic groups tell the story: the Uzbeks in the north are linked culturally and linguistically to Uzbekistan, and they speak a language that belongs to the Turkic family of languages common in central Asia. The Tajiks in the West are linked to Tajikistan, speak a local dialect of Persian called Dari, and they have historically been linked to Persian culture. Other small groups also exist, the most notable of which are the Hazaras in central Afghanistan, who represent the major Shi'ite presence of the population. But all those groups do not amount together to more than half of the population at most, while the Pashtun ethnic groups constitute the single largest group of the population, composing perhaps 40 or 45 percent of the population, if not more. They reside mostly in the south and speak Pashto, which belongs to a family of Indo-Persian languages. But the Pashtuns do not constitute a monolithic group, and they extend in presence to Pakistan. They are split along family tribal lines, and a major tribal confederation split the Pashtuns of Afghanistan into two groups: the Ghilzai and the Durranis, and the external powers (the British and later the Russians) tried their best to exploit and exacerbate these divisions. The exploitation worked—until the Afghanis felt united by enmity toward external invaders. This led the British to comment that it is possible to "rent" the Afghanis, but impossible to buy them. They also have a reputation of toughness: even the Arabs have heard the warning to beware of the venom of the cobra, the teeth of the tiger, and the revenge of the Afghans.

Monarchy emerged under the Durran confederation of the Pashtuns in the 18th century, when a *loya jirga* (or tribal summit) selected a king by acclamation. This was not technically a dynasty, although it lasted until 1973 when King Dhahir Shah was deposed. (He is the same king that the

U.S. desperately tried—and failed—to revive in an attempt to counter-balance the non-Pashtun power base of its friends in the Northern Alliance.)

The British, in competition with the Russians, tried several times to control Afghanistan, to no avail. They were defeated three times, and they eventually gave up and settled into the role of patron. It was only after the 1979 Soviet invasion of the country that the world came to learn about the complexity and uniqueness of Afghanistan. It is now hard to believe that Afghanistan was a major news story for the American press in the 1980s; that Dan Rather donned Afghani clothing and slipped into the country to report to his country about those heroes who were bending the knees of the Soviet Empire, just as Geraldo Rivera "slipped" into Afghanistan post-September 11 and promised to kill bin Laden if he were to find him alive.

The U.S. government pumped weapons and intelligence into the *mujahideen*[41]—an Arabic word which then entered Western consciousness as a synonym of bravery and principle. The lionization did not last; the Soviet Union packed and left in 1989, and the U.S. followed soon thereafter.

The Afghanistan chapter of the Cold War is an important one; we are told that Jimmy Carter did not discover the evil of the Soviet Union until the Soviet invasion of Afghanistan. For his intensely anti-communist National Security Advisor, Afghanistan was an opportunity of a lifetime: to be able to throw in American military and political support, covertly of course, and to rally anti-Communist forces from around the world was an appealing project that would weaken the soft anti-communist voices in the U.S. Congress. The days of détente suddenly belonged to a distant past, and the new Reagan administration, with CIA director William Casey, lunged at the chance to fight the Soviets in Asia and Latin American simultaneously. The struggle was never about the Afghani people; no mention was made of the agenda of the Islamic fundamentalists to whom Saudi Arabia was supplying indoctrination and cash. Nor was mention made of the plight of women; nobody could express any sympathy for the feminist agenda of the Afghani communists lest one becomes accused of supporting the evil empire itself.

Saudi Arabia and its Arab gulf regimes were interested in that struggle for at least two reasons. First, they also feared the spread of communism, which once threatened some Arab governments. King Khalid, who succeeded King Faysal in 1975, was a genuinely devout Muslim who was closely aligned with the militant puritanical forces in Saudi Arabia's clerical establishment. Second, the Saudi royal family was always eager for favors to do for the United States, to bring the two countries closer, and to prove to Washington that Israel was not the only reliable ally of the U.S. in the region. This explains Saudi funding of the Contras, and other Saudi funding for Casey's costly adventures around the world. The new Saudi ambassador in Washington (and the current ambassador, Bandar bin Sultan) was a champion of this school. He desperately wished to demonstrate that Saudi Arabia was more than merely an oil source or a customer with a limitless budget for high-end U.S. weapon systems.

The unity of Islamic fundamentalist factions was only temporary, of course. When the enemy of the *mujahideen* left, ethnic and tribal divisions were quickly restored. The U.S. was too disinterested to step in; Afghanistan was left to its religious fanatics and to the massive supply of weapons that was left by the two super powers. The communist regime was counting its days; its leaders advanced many proposals of compromise and power sharing, but none of them were acceptable to the fighters. Godless communism had to be completely eliminated, and the traditions—which always wound up oppressing women in every culture and religion—had to be restored. The international media left Afghanistan behind, and the daily shelling of Kabul became routine. The heroes of yesterday were quickly forgotten as the U.S. moved forward orchestrating Operation Desert Shield and Operation Desert Storm, i.e., the Gulf War. Russia had the families of her 15,000 dead combatants to remind her of the futility of any new adventures of domination. The Soviet empire was heading toward its own grave, and Islamic rebellions were sprouting within Russia itself.

Changing regional dynamics within Afghanistan could not be overlooked, especially by Pakistan with whom it shares a massive border. Pakistan had India to contend with, and in post-Soviet Afghanistan the nascent forces of Islamic fundamentalist militancy would only advantage Pakistan in its struggle with India over Kashmir.

Kashmir is a predominantly Muslim region in India which the Pakistanis want to annex in the name of Muslim solidarity. The Pakistani government has armed and supported forces fighting for Kashmiri independence. To date, the two giants have three times gone to war over Kashmir. The acquisition of nuclear weapons by both countries is the direct product of the Kashmiri conflict. While Kashmir is a remote foreign policy issue to the United States, it is dear to the hearts of Muslim fundamentalists. Their publications regularly feature reports about the struggle of their brethren in Kashmir. The Kashmiri cause has never inspired any official support from any Arab or Muslim countries, but it has mobilized support from Muslim Brotherhood and their numerous progenies and offshoots. For that reason, the powerful Pakistani military-intelligence apparatus, which has been closely linked to U.S. intelligence and military since at least the 1950s, could not abandon the Afghani scene.

Pakistan seems to have sponsored, if not spawned, the phenomenon of the Taliban (Pashto plural of *talib*, Arabic for student) who seem to have emerged from the misery of refugee camps in Pakistan. Students in those camps were indoctrinated with both anti-communism *and* anti-Americanism. They were taught that the U.S. had used, abused, and abandoned them in the same way that the U.S. had used the rebels of southern Sudan against the northern Arab government in Khartoum, or the Kurds of Northern Iraq who were used in strategies against the central government in Baghdad, among many others.

Significantly, the Taliban were also under the influence of the Wahhabi internationalist campaign that the Saudi royal family had undertaken since at least the the Soviet invasion of Afghanistan, if not earlier. The royal family wanted to win over new converts to the cause, and Central Asia was a new arena for ideological propaganda. When the Soviet Union collapsed, several Muslim governments scrambled to fill the region's political vacuum; Turkey, Iran, and Saudi Arabia each worked to win new converts to their causes. The Taliban's brand of Islam, which raised the ire of many Muslims and non-Muslims alike, was very much in tune with the Hanbalite School of jurisprudence.[42] But the story of Saudi's international Islamism in itself deserves special attention.

The causes of the Pakistani embrace of Taliban are multifaceted. First, the Pakistani dictator Zia ul-Haq, who led the covert CIA campaign against the Soviets in the region, turned militantly Islamist and pious, funneling money and weapons to the extremist religious fundamentalists. This reliable U.S. ally was the one who set up hundreds of militant religious schools from which emerged the early Taliban activists. But even after Zia ul-Haq's death in 1988, Pakistani leadership, especially the ostensibly secular Benazir Bhutto (who recently toured the U.S. to lecture about the evil and misogyny of the Taliban) also endorsed the fundamentalists and supported the Taliban as an opportunity to create a stable pro-Pakistani government that would fend off Iranian Shi`ite influence within Afghanistan.

Pakistan also was biased in favor of rule by Pashtuns. They preferred the Pashtuns to the minority ethnic groups who have been aligned with Iran and are dominant in the Northern Alliance. That the Taliban espoused a militant branch of Islam did not cause much consternation among the leaders of the Pakistani military-intelligence apparatus as they benefitted from the fundamentalists adoption of the Kashmiri cause, which clearly witnessed a resurgence since the *mujahideen* entered that region as fighters for Islam, their brand of Islam of course. The Pakistani government could now send eager fighters to Kashmir without having to worry about links to its military. It now could simply attribute the growing military activity in Kashmir to *jihad* groups that came from different parts of the world.

The Arab *mujahideen*—fundamentalists who came from all around the Arab world, including from the Arabian peninsula—posed a different problem. They stood apart and they never trusted the Americans. Their fighters never rested, and were always on the lookout to open new fronts of struggle. Even after the mysterious assassination of their Palestinian leader `Abdullah `Azzam in 1989, they continued to flourish and spread. They found training grounds for fighters across the Middle East. The Pakistanis knew that they would be difficult to control. From that current emerged a Muslim international that would become an increasing threat to Americans interests at home and abroad.

The "Arab Afghans," as they were called, can be traced back to the charismatic and powerful figure `Abdullah `Azzam. He was the first Arab to see in the Afghani cause an opportunity to evolve an international Islamic network, and there is no question that it was `Azzam who has inspired bin Laden more than anybody else. There were reports that bin Laden had first met `Azzam in Saudi Arabia while the latter was on one of his many fund-raising trips to the Gulf region.

bin Laden was at the time a college student. `Azzam, atypical of Palestinians, did not believe in modern nationalism; in fact, he viewed Arab and Palestinian nationalism as dangerous plots to sew disunity among Muslims. In practice and theory, `Azzam preached an international Islamic solidarity that would create a force to use against Islam's many enemies.[43]

Afghan Arabs were those who heeded the call to arms first by `Azzam, and later by bin Laden. These men were rejects in their own governments; Muslim fundamentalists who were barely acquitted in various court cases of violence, or were fundamentalists who fled their own countries certain that they would be captured and killed. The Egyptian government, due to its brutal campaign of oppression and indiscriminate killing, left large segments of the fundamentalist opposition without any legal or political resorts. Many found haven in the political/religious extreme of Afghanistan. They had to become committed and militant fighters; unlike other fighters there, they had nowhere left to go. Their government did not want them, and other governments were under intense pressure (from Egypt or the U.S.) not to admit them. The group was able to draw from the ranks of dissident Egyptian youth, as well as from the youth of countries that bin Laden frequented: primarily Saudi Arabia and Sudan. Algeria was also a source, as the fundamentalist radicalization of the 1980s and 1990s produced new militants who did not want to live under the rule of the "secular" generals. Many Algerians linked with bin Laden's network later formed the horrific Armed Islamic Group, which became notorious for its brutal methods in the ongoing Algerian civil war.[44]

Meanwhile, Afghanistan's civil war, which was triggered by the Soviet withdrawal from Afghanistan in 1989, continued. The Northern Alliance—a very loose coalition of mostly Tajik and Uzbek forces in control of no more than some 5 percent of the country—pressed on with a propaganda campaign all their own. They felt that they were the true inheritors of the country, that they were the core of the famous *mujahideen* who had triumphed over the infidel Soviet invaders.

Each Northern Alliance leader controlled a small domain based on ethnic and tribal loyalties. The strict obscurantism of the Taliban (who wanted to fight all facets of modernity with more zeal than the Wahhabi clerics of Saudi Arabia) together with their severe misogyny, allowed the Northern Alliance to take advantage of Western attention. They posed as the moderate faction, although they also espoused a fundamentalist version of Islam, and no women sat on their *Shura* (consultation) council. Their charismatic military leader, Ahmad Shah Masoud, who fascinated Western reporters partly because he knew French and appreciated poetry, would maintain that such matters as the realization of women's rights would take time. How long, however, we were never told.

The strength of the Northern Alliance had been severely eroding, but in the immediate aftermath of September 11, they were rediscovered and reborn. Ahmad Shah Masoud was assassinated on September 9, 2001 by two men who had artfully posed as journalists using fake press credentials issued by a London-based fundamentalist now under arrest for alleged links to bin Laden. Conspiracy theorists may forever wonder whether there is a connection between the September 11 attacks and the assassination of Masoud. Regardless, the assassination of Masoud was a severe setback to the Northern Alliance.

Prior to September 11, the Alliance could not muster a force strong enough to dislodge the Taliban, and their short-lived rule over Kabul was so corrupt and cruel that they paved the road for the rise of the purist Taliban. The mystique of Mullah Omar, the Taliban leader, was based in part on the tale of his rescue of two girls who were kidnapped and raped by *mujahideen* fighters. Sexual rape of boys and girls was not uncommon, as was large-scale theft and extortion.[45] To protect cities under their control, and to expand their zone of influence, the armies of the Northern Alliance would indiscriminately bombard cities and villages outside of their control.

The Northern Alliance coalition was so fragmented that it invited foreign sponsors: Iran, Pakistan, India, Russia, and Saudi Arabia all wanted to shape Afghanistan's future in their interest. Thus, Saudi Arabia urged a pro-Saudi Afghan, `Abdul-Rasul Sayyaf to found a Wahhabi party to promote Saudi interests, and thus Ittehad-e-Islami was created in Peshawar. Prince Turki bin Faysal, head of Saudi intelligence for the last 25 years, took keen interest in Afghani affairs, and became well acquainted with bin Laden. He unceremoniously retired—or perhaps was forced to retire—in 2001. In a sense, Turki is the true father of the Arab Afghans.

What remains mysterious is the extent of American involvement in rise of the Taliban. In a recent interview, the former Saudi Ambassador to Afghanistan, maintains that the U.S. was directly involved in the sponsorship of the Taliban because they were anti-Iranians.[46] There is no question that the U.S. tolerated their emergence, and it was no coincidence that three regimes that extended official recognition to the Taliban were all close allies of the U.S.: Saudi Arabia, United Arab Emirates, and Pakistan. None of these regimes withdrew their recognition of Taliban authority over Afghanistan until after September 11. And we have no information regarding American displeasure with the recognitions prior to that date. Furthermore, the U.S. presidential envoy to Afghanistan, Zalmay Khalilzad, who also serves as the National Security Council's lead figure on the Middle East, had lobbied strongly for U.S. cooperation with the Taliban while working for the multinational oil company Unocal, which sponsored the only official visit by Taliban officials to the U.S. prior to September 11. In 1996, Khalilzad defended the Taliban in the *Washington Post*, writing that "the Taliban does [sic] not practice the anti-U.S. style of fundamentalism practiced by Iran. We should...be willing to offer recognition and humanitarian assistance..."[47]

The U.S. seemed to have only two areas of contention with the Taliban: harboring bin Laden and cultivating opium. However, once the Taliban issued a *fatwa* forbidding the cultivation of drugs, the U.S. responded by issuing them several million dollars of reward. Unfortunately, as soon as the Taliban lost control of power in November 2001, news of resumed drug cultivation immediately began emerging.[48]

The war against terrorism will now require the acquisi-

As`ad AbuKhalil

tion of new friends, and a desperate attempt is being made, under Pakistani pressure, to find Pashtun tribes ready to defect from the Taliban cause. This may mean that the U.S. will have to look the other way while their new allies and friends fundraise through drug trafficking. Will the new war on terrorism override the old war on drugs?

4

THE SAUDI CONNECTION

I t's surprising how little press coverage the Saudi connection received in Western media prior to September 11. The Saudis, along with their ally the U.S., have had a primary responsibility for the rise of Islamic fundamentalism worldwide, a connection that developed during the long and turbulent decades of the Cold War. The reason why the Saudis are now under Western scrutiny is because the U.S. no longer has a reason to continue encouraging the growth of radical Islamic fundamentalism, especially since the events surrounding the trial of the assassins of Anwar Sadat in 1981, and more importantly, since the movement has increasingly turned against the United States.

In the context of the Cold War, Saudi Arabia and the U.S. were both worried about their interests in the Middle East, especially during the heyday of Arab nationalism under Jamal Abdul Nasser, who hoped to topple the Saudi royal family, and other pro-Western monarchs in the Middle East in the 1950s and 1960s.[49] While the U.S. was obsessed with the threat of communism internationally, the Saudi royals were focused on maintaining political control internally. During the Cold War years, power was getting shaky for the Saudi royal family, especially before 1964 when King Faysal engineered some reforms in the political system after ousting his own brother. The destabilizing force for the Saudis was Arab nationalism (which seeks to eliminate all borders between Arab nations to create one all-encompassing Arab entity), and the charismatic leadership of Egypt's Jamal Abdul-Nasser. Nasser mocked and fought against all "reactionary regimes" of the region which he dismissed as "tales of colonialism." He succeeded in luring members of the Royal family itself, and the father of Saudi billionaire Al-Walid bin Talal, Prince Talal bin `Abdul-`Aziz, set up shop in Cairo, and was nicknamed the Red Prince.[50] (He now would like to forget this chapter of his life, but those who write the history of modern Arab nationalism still remember him.)

The rebellion in North Yemen in the 1960s, which put an end to royal rule there, and which was strongly supported by Nasser, instilled fear in the hearts of many princes and kings in the region. The threat was imminent, and Saudi and American interests converged. Both wanted to keep the rule of the right-wing monarchs stable; this is what was dubbed as "the stability of the Persian Gulf" in U.S. foreign policy parlance.

It was during that political moment that American and Saudi connections began funding and developing various Islamic fronts to fend off the socialist and Arab nationalist dangers. Initially, the radical Islamic fronts they created were not very credible; the supply of money and arms created little more than a propaganda existence without which they would have sunk into oblivion. The front groups produced a body of books and pamphlets calling on believers to reject atheistic communism and to embrace the path of the "good predecessors," known as *Salaf*, hence the name

Salafiyyah to refer to modern fundamentalists who want to bring back the glory of the early days of Islam. The Taliban are thus *Salafiyyah*, although the goal of attaining glory, of any kind, clearly eluded them.

At first the radical Islamic fronts were very limited in influence; Nasser knew how to discredit them, and his version of progressive Arab nationalism made them look too passé for the enthusiastic masses. However, the groups began to take on a life of their own after Arab armies suffered a humiliating defeat vis-à-vis Israel in 1967. The aftermath of the defeat provoked a process of profound political and intellectual reexamination that further energized Islamic fundamentalism as an oppositional path. In some cases, regimes like Egypt, Jordan, and Israel, directly assisted the fundamentalists in order to subvert the further rise of the left, then at the peak of its influence in the region. What Egypt, Jordan, and Israel could not then know was that the fundamentalists would soon undergo dramatic radicalization in goals and tactics that would later haunt them.

The fundamentalist vision changed after the 1967 Arab defeat. It moved from a conservative social message that emphasized prayer and religious obligations to one that sounded a call for arms under the banner of Islam. The impact of the Arab-Israeli War of 1973 served to further validate the fundamentalist message, while at the same time sinking the left into deeper decline and irrelevance. Saudi Arabia was not a bystander to those developments, it actively continued to fund and sponsor its own brand of fundamentalist Islam at the expense of other less militant strains.

As`ad AbuKhalil

The Saudis created a plethora of Islamic fronts, congresses, and organizations all around the world. Despite all their efforts, the Saudi royalty's quest for Islamic credibility and legitimacy has been an abysmal failure, partly due to their corruption, and partly due to the peculiarities and strictness of the puritanical Islam that they pushed.

Saudi Arabia's version of Islam is particularly harsh and judgmental; it does not fit into the fun-loving lifestyles of the Muslims of the Middle East, many of whom take advantage of loopholes of law and laxity of the applied moral code. The Saudi version of Islam does not receive the attention of more moderate forms in places like Iran or even Sudan; but it is crucial for understanding Osama bin Laden. He, after all, emerged from the womb of Wahhabism and has broken from the royal family of al-Saud, but not from the doctrine itself. In fact, the theological break between bin Laden and the chief Wahhabi cleric bin Baz (more on him later) did not occur until the latter supported the advent of U.S. troops to the kingdom after the Iraqi invasion of Kuwait.[51]

Ninety percent of all Muslims are Sunnis, and most of the rest are Shi`ite.s Within Sunni Islam there are four schools of jurisprudence: the Malikis, the Shafi`is, the Hanafis, and the Hanbalites. The Hanbalite school is named after the strict medieval theologian, Ahmad ibn Hanbal. He withstood torture, refused to renounce his beliefs, and became known as an example of intellectual courage against all odds and pressures. Ibn Hanbal's school, however, was too strict and conservative for most; to this day it is followed only by a very narrow segment of the world's Muslims.

The strictness and extremism of ibn Hanbal appeals to many contemporary Islamic ultra-fundamentalists. His sexism was such that to him was attributed the saying: "everything of the woman is a pudendum (`awrah)," which is not different from some strands of Orthodox Judaism. (This saying was cited in a manual urging women to don the veil, and circulated illegally by al-Jama`ah al-Islamiyyah, the fundamentalist group that used to be headed by Sheik Abdel Rahman, the blind Egyptian cleric who is presently serving time in a U.S. prison for involvement in the 1993 World Trade Center bombing.[52]

The Hanbalite school was energized by the founding of Saudi Arabia in the 20th century. The kingdom was founded on a very delicate alliance between the House of Saud and the clerical establishment that follows the doctrine of Muhmmad ibn `Abdul-Wahhab (1703-1792), after whom the doctrine of Wahhabiyyah is named. In practice, Saudi Arabia adopted the Hanbalite school and made Wahhabiyyah the state religion. As a result, Saudi Arabia's official religious practice is extreme and eccentric, which has distanced it from mainstream Islamic teachings. Now Wahhabiyyah is supposed to be above the four Sunni schools of jurisprudence although its proximity to Hanbalite doctrine is obvious.

Wahhabiyyah is the most extreme form of theoretical or practiced Islam; it is an Islam that fears progress, change, and cross-cultural influences. It is the school of Islamic fundamentalist theology that equates excess with piety, and extremism with virtue, although the Koran urges that "there shall be no compulsion in religion." Of all Muslim

As`ad AbuKhalil

countries, only Saudi Arabia officially follows Wahhabiyyah. Qatar also officially adheres to Wahhabiyyah, but the small emirate has been moving away from it for years, and is currently undergoing serious political openings that are bringing about improvements in women's rights and other social causes. Wahhabiyyah preaches a return to what they view as fundamentals of Islam, and this makes Saudi Arabia perhaps the first Islamic fundamentalist state in the modern Middle East. Wahhabiyyah aims at purifying religion from all "satanic" influences, including most facets of modernity, including for some the use of cameras and modern electronic gadgets. It is obsessed with *tawhid* (professing the unity of God) and abandoning any belief that may be seen as *shirk* (worshipping anything or anybody other than God.)[53]

The king of Saudi Arabia had to cope with a clerical rebellion when TV was first introduced in 1960s, just as the clerics first had objected to the introduction of radio and only changed their minds when shown that radios can be used to propagate the Koran. Wahhabiyyah rejects mysticism and calls for the protection of Muslim youths from the corruptions of Westernization and modernity. The Wahhabi clerical establishment tolerates the royal family's foreign policy and controversial alliance with the U.S. so long as the kingdom's educational institutions are controlled by the fundamentalist clerics, who, while accepting education for females, remain opposed to the integration of women in social and political life. The balance between the two sectors has survived, and the royals have convinced the clerics to accept some vestiges of modernity (radio, TV, etc.). The political quiescence of the clerics is partly due to the reactionary political views of the founder of Wahhabiyyah himself, who preached that "rulers should be obeyed despite their injustice and the harm they do."[54]

For the last 50 years, Saudi Wahhabiyyah has been shaped by the Saudi head of *ifta'* (the council that issues binding religious edicts), `Abdul-`Aziz bin Baz, who until his death in 1999 was the most powerful religious personality in the kingdom. He epitomized the deal that is at the heart of the Saudi regime: he was willing to support the political sustenance of the Saudi royal family provided that he enjoy total independence in matters of education and religious propagation. Until shortly before his death, bin Baz was convinced that the earth was flat, disbelieved the news of the landing on the moon, and even suspected conspiracies behind the propagation of such falsehoods. He banned shaving and cologne, and he prohibited music and singing. It is to this form of rule that we may trace the origins of the Taliban.

Bin Baz also endorsed the doctrine of anti-Shi`ism despite the fact that approximately 20 percent of the kingdom's population were Shi`ites. He preached against intermarrying with Shi`ites, whom he considered infidels. It was bin Baz who was responsible for the ban forbidding women from car driving in Saudi Arabia.[55] He also banned pictures and statues, and the Taliban's destruction of the Buddhist statues in Bamiyan last year demonstrated the influence of his brand of Wahhabi teachings. Bin Baz argued that pictures should be destroyed and that photographers should be cursed, and they will suffer the most after resurrection.[56] Bin Baz also assert-

As`ad AbuKhalil

ed that angels would not step into a house that contained pictures.[57] He even went as far as banning foosball—the soccer board game that uses hand-controlled rods that go through miniature human figures—because the game contains little statues.[58]

Wahhabiyyah's version of Islam insists that the Koran be interpreted literally, which results in the propagation of hindering social taboos. The Wahhabiyyah clerics believe that it is morally safer to preserve the lifestyle and conditions of the early companions of the Prophet, as impractical as this is. This explains why Saudi Arabia is bereft of most forms of entertainment, including movie theatres. And Saudi TV is no more than a compilation of the religious opinions of the clerics mixed with the daily list of guests visiting members of the royal family.

Wahhabiyyah is quite alien to most Islamic practitioners, and it makes Ayatollah Ruhallah Khomeini of the Iranian Revolution look modern and lenient by comparison. The phobia that overwhelms Wahhabi theology concerns perceived threats to the strict monotheism of Islam. In response to that perception, the clerics of Wahhabiyyah have created an expansive category of prohibitions, and are responsible for the feared morality police in Saudi Arabia, later emulated in Afghanistan by the Taliban in the name of the Committee for the Promotion of Virtue and the Prohibition of Vice. Wahhabiyyah cannot be sure as to whether the modern innovations in people's lives are satanic in origin or not, so they tend to ban them altogether just to be safe. The Saudi royal family permits the clerics to preach and propagate this brand of fundamentalist Islam as long as they themselves do not have to adhere to them. Until his incapacitation, King Fahd lived the high life; CIA reports have described his alcoholic ways.[59]

The crisis between the royals and the clerics first surfaced in the late 1970s. The Iranian Revolution, although a Shi`ite revolution, changed the political map of the Middle East and brought a new level of religious fervor to the region. The prospects of a fundamentalist seizure of power were suddenly real, and the implications of the Iranian Revolution immediately redefined U.S. foreign policy throughout the region. During the Cold War, Iran's dictatorial leader was considered a trusted ally who was willing to defy his country's political and religious sensibilities in return for lavish U.S. protection and military aid. The Iranian Shah was willing to take up the fight against communism in Iran and throughout the Middle East. The Shah used his forces in internal oppression in places like Oman and Jordan, and bent to U.S. interests when it came to oil policies and pricing.[60]

Although Wahhabiyyah Saudis publish a wide array of anti-Shi`ite propaganda, the religious youths in the kingdom, especially those in Wahhabiyyah-run schools, were energized by the Iranian Revolution. A rebellion of religious students led by Juhayman al-`Utaybi took over the Great Mosque in Mecca in 1979. His outlook was not dissimilar to that of bin Laden. There is no record of what bin Laden thought of al-`Utaybi, who was instantly killed. Foreign troops had to be imported to crush the rebellion. Afterwards, the royals and clerics were no longer easily reconciled: the lifestyles and corruption of the royal family were inconsistent with the puritanical message of Wahhabiyyah. A breach became imminent. To appease the clerics, the government gave them more power and privilege, which led to an increase of religious indoctrination in schools and an increase of funding for international religious schools sponsored by the clerics. But the rebellion of pious al-`Utaybi struck a cord: he openly exposed the corruption and hypocrisy of the princes that would no longer be a secret in Saudi popular and religious circles. Furthermore, support for holy struggles in the Muslim world would thereon be augmented, and Afghanistan presented a cause in which the focus of the clerics and the U.S. government overlapped. For all concerned, fighting against the Soviets in Afghanistan was an opportunity not to be missed.

The Saudi role funding the *mujahideen* expressed the fundamentalist ideals from which the kingdom was founded. The clerics were pleased to see Saudi Arabia supporting brothers in arms fighting against "infidel" Soviets. Some members of the royal family took personal interest in the cause; King Khalid, who was succeeded by the hedonist King Fahd, was not the only pious member of the family. Charity for holy causes mushroomed around the region, and the conflict with Iran catalyzed support for international causes as a counter-force to ambitious Iranian designs. It was in this context that the Saudis later embraced the Taliban: they were the beneficiaries of Saudi political funding from the anti-communism years. Saudi Arabia was also hoping to spread its influence into Central Asia. Regional governments had been warning for years about Wahhabiyyah movements and organizations, particularly the Islamic Movement of Uzbekistan. The United States did not counter the Saudi's support of the Taliban, as it was increasingly interested in extending a natural gas pipeline through Afghanistan, and the cooperation of a stable force in Afghanistan—the Taliban—was essential.

5

THE RISE OF OSAMA BIN LADEN

In many ways, the story of Osama bin Laden is the story of Saudi foreign policy spiraling out of control. He is a member of a prestigious Saudi family that has been closely aligned with the royal family since the days of the founding king. He preaches the same fundamentalist branch of Islam that is taught in Saudi schools. It is the royals who have deviated, not him, as he argues to his Arab audiences. Bin Laden's Saudi supporters understand his denunciations of the desecration of the holy places by "infidel" armies of "Jews and Crusaders"—bin Laden always calls Christians "crusaders" as some Saudi clerics do—his denunciations of Saudi's evil link with American interests, and the Royal family's betrayal of Islam. In fact, one of the signatures of bin Laden's thought is his crude and vulgar discourse regarding his enemies. He never expresses hostility to Israel as Israel, or even to Zionism. He makes it clear that what he hates are all Jews; just as his rhetoric against "crusaders" seems to be hate speech directed to all Christians. Soon after the success against the Soviets in Afghanistan, his speech turned against his fellow Saudis in order to drive deeper the wedge between the clerics and the royals.

Osama bin Laden was born in Riyadh in 1957[61] (*Time* magazine says 1956 or 1958). His Yemeni father, Muhammad

`Awad bin Laden, left Hadramawt, Yemen in 1930 to work as
a porter in Jidda. He quickly rose in the construction business
and made a fortune during the kingdom's early boom years.
He won the contract that expanded the kingdom's Holy
Mosques, and built palaces for the royal family. It is also
believed that he was behind the repair of the Aqsa mosque in
Jerusalem after it was damaged by a blaze.[62]

Muhammad `Awad bin Laden died in a plane crash in
1970. Osama was number 43 among the surviving siblings, and 21st among the sons. It is not known whether
his mother is Syrian or Saudi, as no accessible public documentation exists. His father married at least 10 women,
and Osama may have been a son by the last wife. Western
coverage of his biography describes a youth of indulgences
and corruption. But there is absolutely no evidence of
that. In fact, he was most probably religious at an early
age. The Arabic newspaper *al-Quds al-`Arabi*, which had
access to bin Laden over the years (even though its editor
is a secular Palestinian) found a picture of him in his teens
which was subsequently published in the December 2001
issue of *Vanity Fair*. The photo shows bin Laden—beard-
less and grinning—accompanying his siblings on a trip to
Sweden. He apparently gravitated toward fundamentalism
while in college at King `Abdul-`Aziz University—bin
Laden insists on naming it Riyadh University to avoid rec-
ognizing the rule of al-Saud—in Riyadh in the 1970s,
where he studied management and administration. It is
thought that it was while there that he met the influential
Palestinian fundamentalist and *mujahideen* recruiter,

As`ad AbuKhalil

`Abdullah `Azzam. It is also believed that it was while away at college that he began studying the work of Sayyid Qutb, whose writings deeply influenced bin Laden's religious views.[63]

Sayyid Qutb, an influential fundamentalist thinker and agitator, was arrested by Egypt's Nasser regime and executed in 1966. Unfortunately for his secular opponents, his body of writing survives and continues to inspire Islamic fundamentalists throughout the world. His most famous contribution was his *takfir* method. A *kafir* in Arabic is an infidel or unbeliever, and to declare *takfir* is to ascertain who is the unbeliever in the midst. But Sayyid Qutb was not talking about the declaration of the infidelity of non-Muslims; he was speaking about fellow Muslims. His writings assert that people could be unbelievers even if they were practicing Muslims. Thus, a Muslim society like Egypt could be said to be a corrupt infidel society if the proper Islamic laws (as interpreted by Qutb and his followers of course) are not officially practiced.[64] Qutb went so far as to compare the secular governments under which Muslims live to the pre-Islamic pagan conditions in Arabia. Thus, in Qutb's vision, the killing of fellow Muslims is easily rationalized. For some of his interpreters, it is a duty to engage in such acts because through them the arrival of a truly Muslim society can be realized.

It is not difficult to see the influence of Qutb on bin Laden's actions and organization. Ayman al-Zawahiri, the second in command in the al-Qaeda group, is an Egyptian fundamentalist who officially became an activist right after Qutb's execution.[65]

Ayman al-Zawahiri's philosophy is even more militant than that of Qutb's. He steered his group, Islamic Jihad, in the most fanatic and violent possible direction, and coordinated a horrific massacre of tourists on Egyptian soil. It was Ayman al-Zawahiri's vision that provided the theological and political philosophy for the alliance between the Egyptian Islamic Jihad, which he heads, and bin Laden's al-Qaeda. The alliance between the groups was cemented on February 23, 1998 when they jointly announced the founding of The International Islamic Front for the Combat of Jews and Crusaders.

During the war against the Soviets in Afghanistan, bin Laden's reputation was built more from his organizational than his military skill. He utilized his public administration degree by keeping a record of all the Arabs who passed through Afghanistan, a project that grew out of his initial displeasure with the lack of information about Arab visitors and fighters, especially when Arab mothers would call inquiring about their missing sons. He later used this record to database a large international network of fighters and volunteers. Militarily, he did not establish a distinguished record, although it is said that his personal AK-47 was captured from a Soviet soldier that he had killed. One visitor to `Azzam in 1984 reported that bin Laden was constantly shuttling between Jidda and Afghanistan, and that he was not assigned any one military role.[66]

Osama bin Laden was, in fact, not originally an enemy of

the Saudi government. He fought in Afghanistan and maintained good ties with members of the royal family, many of whom fund raised on behalf of the Afghani cause. That his family was closely tied to the government gave Osama both special protection and a degree of legitimacy. Using his access to resources, large sums of money, and a network of fighters that he was tracking in Afghanistan, he quickly established his own following. His troubles with the regime began with the invasion of Kuwait and the subsequent Gulf War of 1990-1991, but his citizenship was not revoked, curiously enough, until 1994.

The kingdom's decision to "invite" U.S. troops (although U.S. troops arrived before the official invitation did) was a very controversial one in Saudi Arabia, especially among the clerics, and even within the royal family. According to Bob Woodward's published account, the crown prince was weary and warned the king that U.S. troops may never leave Saudi territory once they arrived.[67] Many clerics considered it an intolerable sacrilege for American troops to even step foot on the same soil that hosted the holy mosques of Mecca and Medina. Of all branches of Islamic adherence, Wahhabiyyah's is the least tolerant toward Christians, Jews, and non-Sunni Muslims. How could Wahhabiyyah be tolerant of Jews and Christians in Saudi Arabia when it considers Shi`ite Islam to be blasphemous? In fact, citizens of Saudi Arabia are forbidden from being members of the Jewish and Christian faith, and one Lebanese Christian, Jamil Barudi, who represented Saudi Arabia in the UN in the 1950s, had to convert to Islam before being permitted to do his job.

With the collapse of the USSR and the end of the Cold War, the United States was seen as the last great evil power standing, and Osama bin Laden focused his energies on it and his home countries. To bin Laden, the U.S. is responsible for the perpetuation of corrupt Saudi rule. In fact, it is doubtful that the Saudi royals would have survived Nasser and the turmoil of the 1960s had it not been for direct British and U.S. support. Nasser was the antithesis of everything Saudi: he promoted a progressive and socialist Islam, and sponsored a kind of state-run feminism. Furthermore, Nasser was willing to use the military-intelligence apparatus against his enemies, especially the fundamentalists who tried to kill him in 1954. And what is very interesting in bin Laden's case, is the extent to which his struggle is a nationalistic rather than ecumenical one.

After being stripped of his Saudi citizenship, bin Laden was fortunate to find shelter in Sudan between 1991 and 1996. Sudan at the time was under the sway of the magnetic personality of Hasan Turabi, who holds degrees from Oxford and Sorbonne, and is the guru of Islamic fundamentalist groups worldwide. His impeccable command of French, English, and Arabic has made him a speaker of international fame. Having studied both classical Islamic jurisprudence and Western civil laws, Turabi consulted with many governments on how to Islamize their laws. In the Muslim world, Turabi is the man to know, and he and bin Laden seemed to really hit it off. More importantly, the friendship between the two men transformed bin Laden: it elevated him from a marginal Saudi dissident to an international figure who was endorsed by one of most esteemed leaders of the Islamic world.

Bin Laden's change in stature did not protect him. Under intense international pressure, Sudan expelled him in 1996, and he returned to Afghanistan and the harsh terrain with which he was familiar. Bin Laden's return also coincided with the spread of the Taliban's influence and their control of Kabul. It is not difficult to imagine the basis of the new alliance: the Taliban must have appreciated bin Laden's militancy and resources, while bin Laden appreciated the safe haven for his growing base of business, religious, and military operations.

Bin Laden espouses an extreme model of government. In his statements to *al-Quds al-`Arabi*, perhaps the only Arab publication not under the influence of oil money, although it has been linked to Yemen, Iraq and Arafat on different occasions, bin Laden praises Taliban application of *shari`ah*, or Islamic laws. What appears to Westerners and to many Muslims as severe interpretations of Islamic penal code, is for bin Laden the representation of the true Islam. The message was clear to Muslims that Mullah Omar, presumably with bin Laden's blessings if not urging, was striving for the Islamic utopia for which Muslim fundamentalists have been struggling for decades.

Bin Laden does not reject the Saudi royal family on the basis of their official religion, but on the basis of their compromised foreign policy and inability to rule the kingdom from a position of authentic Islamic authority. In November 2001, the former head of Saudi intelligence reported to the pro-Saudi MBC TV that bin Laden approached the royal family after the Iraqi invasion of Kuwait, and presented a plan for the defense of the kingdom without incorporating Western troops. Bin Laden was disillusioned by the royal family's action from the Gulf War onward, and with the clerical establishment's lack of resistance to the presence of U.S. troops after 1990.

Misrepresentations of bin Laden abound. For example, he is sometimes portrayed as an ally of Saddam Hussein,[68] though he clearly despises Hussein's secular leadership and brutal persecution of fundamentalists in Iraq. He is also sometimes portrayed as a supporter of the Lebanese Shi`ite Party of God,[69] despite the fact that his group considers Shi`ites to be infidels, and his unofficial spokesperson Abu Qatada[70] calls them *rawafid*—literally, rejectionists, but it has been a pejorative term applied by some Sunnis to Shi`ites.

Based on his own statements, Osama bin Laden's world view is hateful and violent. The text of the 1998 declaration of the Front against Jews and Crusaders is a hateful message against all Westerners. He has on record advocated the killing of American civilians, and in the interview with *Time* magazine and *al-Quds al-`Arabi* he accepts the inevitable death of fellow Muslims that results from acts of Islamic violence. He openly advocates violence against civilians, and his listing of the Arab civilian deaths from Israeli and American acts is clearly intended to justify and incite retaliation against the same.

Despite mass media coverage of militant fundamentalist demonstrations in support of bin Laden, there is no evidence of wide support in the Arab world for the terrorism of September 11. Yet, many in the region seem to admire his defiance and his uncompromising opposition to the U.S.— an admiration that is not surprising, given the subservience of most Arab governments toward Washington.

6

SEPTEMBER 11: VIEWS FROM THE
MIDDLE EAST AND MUSLIM WORLD

The Middle East braced itself when the first news of the September 11 arrived. al-Jazeera television channel[71]—now avidly watched throughout the Arabic speaking world—delivered the horrendous news. Al-Jazeera breaks Middle Eastern governments' monopoly over news dissemination and provide an indigenous alternative to the BBC and Radio Monte Carlo, which for years were the reliable sources of news for millions of Arabs.[72] Middle Easterners braced themselves on September 11 because they know that there would be no international mechanisms nor internal American opposition powerful enough to restrain a violent U.S. response.

Early reports were sketchy, and many Arabs refused to believe that those responsible were also Arab. Many could not believe that 19 Arabs with rudimentary English would be able to pull off such a sophisticated and audacious attack. Conspiracy theories spread like wild fire, and both Arabic and Pakistani media published articles reporting that no Jewish people showed up for work at the World Trade Center on the morning of the 11th, accusing Israel's Mossad as the ones responsible for the act. Of course, the reports were false, and the exaggeration of the roles of Mossad and other foreign intelligence agencies in the Middle East seemed to foster a mood of defeatism and diminished political will. Yet, Middle East media still confidently "report" that grotesque conspiracy theory.

The early coverage of the Middle East showed gloating in Pakistan, Lebanon, and Palestine. Arafat was embarrassed by the celebrations of the tragedy, and countered by donating his own blood, footage of which aired in the West. CNN's clip showing Palestinians dancing in the streets was challenged as being archival footage, years old. But the footage was authentic. There was also Arab and Pakistani coverage of gloating, and the Lebanese press carried many pictures and videos of Palestinians and Lebanese celebrating.

Years of open American political, military, and economic favoritism toward Israel—a country that invaded Lebanon—is a bias that has created equally strong counter-biases. The unbalanced attention that Israeli victims of violence receive in the U.S. always strikes Middle Easterners as examples of racial and ethnic preference. American leaders (including President Bill Clinton) have travelled to Israel to show sympathy and solidarity in the wake of terrorist attacks there, yet it is inconceivable for U.S. presidents to show sympathy for Palestinians or Arabs or Muslims when they are targets of terrorist acts. George Bush will not even meet with Yasser Arafat in the White House. Yet, Israel's militant far-right prime minister visited George Bush's White House at least four times during Bush's first year in office. These counterbiases were only reinforced when the U.S. ignored the plight of Afghanistan's people after the withdrawal of Soviet troops, when the civil war in that country was agitated by the U.S. and fought with American weapons.

It is also important not be dragged along the U.S. standards of outrage even when one abhors the terrorism of September 11. One can be outraged at the cruelty of the bombings without necessarily agreeing with the implicit American view that American deaths are more tragic than another's. The more than 3,000 people who perished in the September 11 attacks were from all races, ethnicities, and religions. It was a crime against humanity. Yet, an average of 5,000 children die every month in Iraq as a result of U.S. sanctions, according to studies conducted by the United Nations Children's Fund (UNICEF). Will the tragedy of America's recent loss help it to identify with the suffering it causes around the world and act to eradicate it? Are the preventable deaths of thousands of defenseless children less a crime against humanity than the attacks of September 11? It is easy for European powers and the U.S. to dismiss the death and suffering of poor people in non-European countries by invoking the repulsive clichés about how "they do not value human life the way we do" or by making offensive and ignorant references to "other religions" that do not have the same sanctity of human life the way "we do." Such clichés are not dead, but are still invoked, and they strike people of the Middle East and Asia as infused with a tinge of past colonial thinking.

The Middle East is a region where democratic representation is the exception, not the norm, and Cyprus—not Israel—may be the only true democracy in the area.[73] Middle Eastern governments that assure the U.S. of their

As`ad AbuKhalil

support are governments that are not selected by their own people. The pronouncements of the King of Jordan, whose family ruled the country initially through British colonial support and later through direct American intervention, barely represent the opinions of the royal family. And General Musharraf of Pakistan is a military dictator who appointed himself as president and who is precariously balancing American demands for military support with the angry public opinion of his nation. The people of the Middle East and Asia—indeed, the people of the world—have every right to wonder why some acts of violence are punished and why other acts are left unpunished, and why some acts of violence are even rewarded.

It is indubitable that the U.S. government over the years has rewarded Israeli violent oppression of Palestinians and Lebanese because it was seen as part of a legitimate fight against "terrorism." The first witness-expert on terrorism to appear before Congress in the wake of the bombing was none other than former Israeli prime minister Benjamin Netanyahu, who was personally responsible for giving orders that resulted in the deaths of scores of innocent Lebanese and Palestinians. What public schools or media educated Americans of the 15,000 Lebanese and Palestinians (mostly civilians) who died in the 1982 Israeli invasion of Lebanon? The dark pages of American foreign policy history simply do not exist in the minds of Americans.

7

AMERICA'S WAR AGAINST TERRORISM

As the U.S. government engages in its new war on terrorism abroad, it is altering the domestic agenda at home. On September 11, anchorman Tom Brokaw called on Americans to "reconsider our liberties," and Supreme Court Justice Sandra O'Connor has since warned that we may see the most severe curtailment of our civil liberties ever. America's mood has been vengeful, and the suspension of rights seems to not to concern the majority of people. Groups like the ACLU and the Center for Constitutional Rights have been speaking out, but few seem to be willing to break step with the war drums and criticize the government. Anti-war perspectives are simply not part of national discourse. According to a *USA Today* poll, approximately 49 percent of the population supports issuing special ID cards to citizens of Arab descent. The Governor of New Jersey bluntly asked the police in his state to be on the lookout for Arab looking men; and some pilots and passengers have refused to allow Middle East looking men to board their planes. Even an Arab-American Secret Service agent who is part of the president's security detail was kicked out of a plane; the airline later explained that not only was he Arab but he also was reading *The Crusaders Through Arab Eyes* (a great book by French-Lebanese writer Amin Maalouf). The injustice and psychological violence of racial profiling are spiking to unprecedented heights.

From a historical perspective, America's new war against terrorism is not new at all. Didn't the U.S. bomb Libya in 1986 under the pretext of fighting terrorism? Didn't the CIA plant a car bomb in the southern suburbs of Beirut in 1985 to assassinate a Shi`ite religious leader? (They missed their target—Shaykh Muhammad Husayn Fadlallah—but they got 285 other people, innocent civilians, 85 of whom died).[74] Aren't the sanctions imposed against Iraq justified in order to prevent Saddam Hussein from terrorizing his neighbors? Didn't the Reagan administration bomb Lebanon in the 1980s in its fight against terrorism? Weren't Nicaraguan harbors mined in the 1980s because Nicaragua was engaged in terrorism? Hasn't American support for Israel been in order to defend that country from terrorism? And finally, weren't fundamentalist fanatics in Pakistan and Afghanistan armed and financed by the CIA because their common enemy was exporting terrorism?

Clearly, it would be more accurate to view what is happening as a new stage in a war that has been going on for decades. If the past is any indication, it is not unreasonable to fear this new stage, nor to brace oneself for new civilian casualties. Bill Clinton ordered the bombing of a medicine factory in Sudan in 1998, even though, according to Seymour Hersh, his own military commanders were opposed because the evidence was so flimsy. It was later revealed that the U.S. government lied when it claimed that the factory had financial ties to bin Laden, and that it was producing chemical weapons. Despite the devastation caused by its error, the U.S. neither apologized nor offered compensation to the victims of its bombing.

Many questions remain. The president repeatedly states that you are either "with us" or "against us," on the side of "good" or on the side of "evil." Ironically, bin Laden agrees: in his first public statement after September 11, he maintained that "these events have split the entire world into two abodes: an abode of belief where there is no hypocrisy, and an abode of unbelief, may God protect us and you from it."[75] Both bin Laden and Bush reject the possibility of a third camp. Why? What about the people of the Middle East—perhaps a majority of them—who are opposed to both Osama bin Laden and George Bush? Many abhor the indiscriminate violence of al-Qaeda, but also fiercely oppose U.S. actions and policies of the region. And this Manichean vision is increasingly pitting the U.S. government against the Muslim and Arab world, despite the assertion by Bush and other American officials that its war is not against the Islamic faith. Yet what Americans must understand is that all rhetorical devices of the administration evaporate in the face of civilian Muslims killed by U.S. bombs, including children like the 10-year-old son of Mullah Omar, or the wife and children of Ayman al-Zawahiri. Meanwhile, Mullah Omar and al-Zawahiri are still alive. To a large degree, the forces that drive followers of figures like bin Laden into being are the death and suffering of people, directly or indirectly, by the United States and allies it dominates. Changing those policies, something that is ostensibly in the hands of the people, would radically improve conditions for millions of people around the world, and would create a context for peace and security which cannot be

As`ad AbuKhalil

achieved through military campaigns. In the indefinite interim, Muslims will continue to regard the suffering of their brethren as anti-Muslim violence, and anti-Americanism, in all its forms, will grow more virulent.

George Bush insists that his government is not against Muslims or Arabs, but when he first announced a list of 27 groups and individuals that he accused of having terrorist links, all 27 groups were Arab or Muslim.[76] (Only later did they add on non-Arab and non-Muslim groups. Somebody must have alerted them.) The IRA will of course continue to hold fundraisers on American soil, though it is unthinkable that the U.S. will order bombing raids against terrorist bases in Northern Ireland. Basque and Corsican terrorists have nothing to fear. Weapons and money will continue to flow to Israel while it continues its war against the Palestinians. Only when Israel goes too far (i.e. when hundreds are killed in one day, like during the Israeli invasion of Lebanon, or the Sabra and Shatila massacres in 1982) will U.S. officials express reservations publicly, but never to the point of labeling Israeli acts as terrorist.

Despite everything George Bush says to the contrary, news of attacks against Arab and Muslim Americans reported in the Persian, Pakistani, and Arabic press reinforces Middle Eastern perceptions of American bigotry. It may not be fair to blame the American public for the acts of the government, but it certainly is fair to blame the U.S. government and its law enforcement agencies for its heavy use of racial profiling of Arab and Muslim Americans before and after the bombings of September 11. In the sweep of arrests that followed the bombings, more than 1,200 Arabs and Muslims were arrested. The government has since admitted that only one of those arrested have ties to the hijackers. One Saudi cardiologist from San Antonio was flown to New York City and interrogated, only to be released a few days later after it became clear that he knew none of the hijackers. SWAT teams stormed a room where three Arab women were staying at a Boston Hotel because they were related to a man whose name was confused by the FBI with the the last name of one of the 9-11 hijackers. Can the U.S. be expected to change its double standards in dealing with the Middle East? Will victims in Bangladesh suddenly receive the same sympathy that European victims receive in U.S. culture? Will we now remember the innocent civilians who accidentally perished in Muslim countries, or in any other developing countries, the way Princess Diana is eternally remembered?

What are the ideological underpinnings of this war against terrorism? What will the moral justification be? In his highly praised speech to Congress, President Bush invoked human rights, and even listed some violations committed by the Taliban, including their mistreatment of women. Why now? The Taliban have been on the scene since the early 1990s, and their abysmal human rights record and views on women have been known for years. The U.S. has been well aware support for them coming from Pakistan, Saudi Arabia, and the United Arab Emirates, all U.S. allies. Furthermore, the U.S. government had recently rewarded the Taliban for their eradication of the drugs from

As`ad AbuKhalil

territories under their control. Why didn't human rights figure into the government's policy making at the time? Or are human rights only used when convenient, as in the way that George Bush senior cited reports by Amnesty International describing human rights violations committed by Saddam Hussein's regime, but only after Saddam threatened U.S. energy interests by invading Kuwait?

If the U.S. government is truly going to be an advocate for human rights, will we see statements of condemnation against its allies? Will the U.S. utter a word against the Saudi royal family? Will we hear members of congress calling on the loyal king to allow women in his country to drive their own cars? And if the Northern Alliance is going to serve as a major vehicle for U.S. policy in Afghanistan, will their record come under official scrutiny? Surely policy makers know of the human rights violations and drug trafficking committed by the Northern Alliance. In Mazar-i-Sharif alone they massacred hundreds. The central Asian republics are also playing important roles in U.S. policy, and so long as Tajikistan and Uzbekistan serve as staging grounds for U.S. forces, their regimes' record of oppression—denounced by groups like Human Rights Watch and others—will not be officially condemned.

Denunciations of violence against civilians serve as a basis to justify the war. Meanwhile, the U.S. continues to reject Arab and Muslim demands for an international conference on terrorism needed to work out universal definitions and standards. To be sure, Arab governments themselves are guilty of labeling Israeli atrocities as terrorist, while refusing to label their own killing of civilians as terrorist. Arab regimes like Egypt, Iraq, Syria, Jordan, Algeria, Libya, and Saudi Arabia have all engaged in acts of terrorism against their own citizens or against their opponents. They are guilty of the same double standards as the U.S. and Israel. But Arab governments and organizations are justified in requesting a universal agreement on the meaning of terrorism. By current Israeli standards of terrorism, for example, Nelson Mandela is the leader of a terrorist organization.

More importantly, how can the U.S. eradicate anti-U.S. terrorism when there is a consensus in its political culture not to review its foreign policies? It is odd that there are no voices in the mainstream calling for a broad reconsideration of U.S. policy abroad. Such calls are met with indignant refusal to succumb to terrorist pressures. A critical analysis of U.S. foreign policy is often equated with sympathy for terrorist causes. This explains why Barbara Lee of Oakland-Berkeley, CA, was the only voice in the U.S. House of Representatives opposed to increasing the president's unilateral authority to order violence against enemies.

Such a climate discourages an examination of the underlying causes of anti-Americanism in all its forms, the most desperate of which is terrorism. In other words, eradicating terrorism involves an examination of how U.S. foreign policy is linked to oppression and human rights violations abroad. Anything less will fail to improve the climate of resentment and antipathy that is responsible for the attacks of September 11. The emphasis on one group or another can only succeed in dealing with extreme manifestations of

As`ad AbuKhalil

deeper unaddressed issues. The U.S. continues to swat down individual waves while ignoring the growing undertow that creates them.

Anti-American activism caused by resentment of U.S. policy is open and pervasive in the Middle East. To improve the climate, Americans need to bypass commercial media and become aware of the core grievances held against U.S. policy. First, the U.S. is held directly responsible for the imposition of oppressive regimes against the wishes of their people. It is unlikely that the Jordanian, Egyptian, Kuwaiti, Bahraini, Tunisian, and Moroccan regimes would have survived until today if it was not for direct U.S. military, intelligence, and political support. And despite the lofty language of human rights and democracy during Carter's administration and beyond, the people of the Middle East know better. They understand that the U.S. support is based purely on economic and military considerations, and that those interests are fundamentally at odds with democratization and human rights. So when U.S. officials speak about "moderate" and "friendly" Arab governments, the American public needs to realize the people living under those governments do not find them moderate or friendly. But moderation and friendliness are defined purely in terms of subservience to U.S. interests, not the interests of the country's civil society. For example, a Middle East country's willingness to forgive Israel for its mistreatment of Palestinians always earns a "moderate" and "reasonable" label from Washington. The Egyptian dictator Anwar Sadat, who is remembered in America as a statesman, is a good example. His pro-Nazi and anti-Semitic pronouncements were all forgiven because he was willing to expel the Soviets from Egypt and follow American dictates, and eventually sign a peace treaty with Israel. Unlike the short attention span in America, the people of the Middle East do not easily forget, and history of U.S. support for policies that oppress breeds resentment and rage.

Americans need also to realize that the Arab world sympathizes with the people of Iraq even while they reject Saddam Hussein. The anger over the continuing suffering in Iraq receives a large amount of press in the Arab world. U.S. sanctions are held accountable for ongoing civilian suffering and deaths. Even Iraq's regional enemies are now expressing token sympathy for the people of Iraq because they know that their plight is foremost on the minds of their citizens. It is in this context that terrorism wins recruits and makes a case for itself in terms of self-defense and revenge.

Washington's "new" war against terrorism will have long-lasting impact. It is likely to further stigmatize the image of Palestinians, Arabs, and Muslims, as it is likely to portray Palestinian resistance to Israeli occupation and subjugation as terrorism. Israel will continue to receive U.S. money and weapons. The Pentagon will get the defense budget it wants, and more, and no questions will be asked.

The U.S. government is fighting more than one war. In addition to the war in Afghanistan, and its covert ramifications elsewhere, the war against civil liberties will continue domestically. The extensive campaign to "interview" thousands of Arab visitors to the U.S. continues. The Attorney General and the president extracted more powers from the

Congress through the passage of the aptly named USA PATRI-OT Act, an acronym that stands for Uniting and Strengthening America by Providing Appropriate Tools Required to Intercept and Obstruct Terrorism Act.

In the name of patriotism, the rights of Arabs and Muslims in America are being reduced and challenged, and physical harassment and attacks have shot up. The climate of conformity has afflicted popular and academic culture. Voices of dissent are scant and disagreement with the government, according to the December 2001 testimony by Aschcroft before the Senate Judiciary Committee, may aid terrorism. Intimidation of the left and the anti-war movement has been more or less successful.

CONCLUSION

The war will expand. The Taliban movement appears crushed and regional concentrations of al-Qaeda have slipped over the border, or melted into to local communities. American "advisors" have already landed in the Phillipines, and the Deputy secretary of defense has advocated bombing Iraq and Syria. He even stated that the U.S. will "end states" that sponsor terrorism. He did not clarify his remarks. How do states get ended? And what happens to the people of ended states? Do they get relocated to safe havens or do they get "ended" too? There are no answers to these questions.

The release of the latest bin Laden video confirmed in the minds of the public the guilt of bin Laden, as if it was ever in doubt. But the release of the tape was also intended to convince Muslim and Arab audiences. It did not help that the Arab public did not watch the tape with the same interest as the U.S. public. Of course, the image of bin Laden in the tape fits his character. He appears as the callous and cynical fanatic that he has always been. The translation of the tape, which is spotty and reveals deep ignorance of basic Islam on the part of the U.S. translators, speaks volumes about the incompetence of the official U.S. Middle East experts.

The U.S. is not trying to ignore Arab public opinion, it is trying to manipulate it. In a meeting with U.S. Jewish leaders, the *New York Times* reports (December 14, 2001) that when a participant said that there was a need to control the anti-American, anti-Israeli media in the region, Mr. Bush offered assurances, according to one participant, that the United States was sending the message behind the scenes to Arab governments that they needed to control their media. Cheney and Powell appealed directly to the Amir of Qatar to restrain al-Jazeera, the 24-hour Arab satellite channel, that Bush calls "a big one." So much for U.S. promotion of freedoms around the world.

The brutal Israeli campaign against the Palestinians in December 2001 followed a crucial meeting between the Israeli prime minister Sharon and President Bush. The U.S. then used its veto power, for the 24th time in recent decades, to obstruct the passage of a balanced UN Security Council resolution that deployed international monitors in Palestinians areas. The war against terrorism prevents the protection of Palestinian civilians.

The U.S. has certainly dominated in the initial military phase of the campaign. But responses are sure to follow, regardless of whether bin Laden is killed or survives. U.S. military actions are certain to produce more angry youths and more angry clerics and leaders, just as successive Israeli oppression of Palestinians has not succeeded in ending the violent methods of struggle by Palestinians. To quote a *New York Times* cover story, "there are legions of young men who seethe with resentment at America and its power, and long after Mr. bin Laden and al-Qaeda have faded into history, they seem likely to form a ready pool of recruits for messianic leaders." (John F. Burns, January 27, 2002)

The war against terrorism will likely not come to a clear end. It could drag on for years, if not decades. The U.S. may be so eager to slay "the terrorists" that it may ensure the war's extension, as "great powers" tend to do, to quote Paul Kennedy.

The war against terrorism may eventually result in the withdrawal of the U.S. from the Middle East and parts of Asia. Antipathy to U.S. interests is so widespread, that the ability of the U.S. to maintain influence and troops in the region may exceed the threshold of support of the U.S. population.

Pakistan will be in a difficult a position for a long time to come. The military regime is cautious; it must appease the U.S. without losing control of the already agitated street. Pakistan's all-powerful Inter-Services Intelligence apparatus (ISI) will watch developments with a perspective of its own, which may or may not coincide with that of the ruling general. It was the ISI that feverishly cultivated—if not created—the Taliban, managed the conflict with India, and sponsored the fundamentalist groups Army of the Righteous and Army of Muhammad and their armed struggle in Kashmir. The conflict and instability in Afghanistan could easily spread to Pakistan, and the concerns over lack of democracy there does not, of course, trouble policy makers, who gave the signals to the IMF to reward the military rule for its subservience to Washington.

There was a unique moment of opportunity for the U.S. to improve foreign policy after the September 11 attacks, but the president was immediately intent to "kick their asses," as he put it.[77] The U.S. could have seized the moment and capitalized on world's sympathy to present a real formula for the empowerment of international institutions capable of eradicating violence and terrorism worldwide. In fact, a little-noticed plea was made by the most prominent Islamic and Islamist thinkers and writers in the Muslim world right after September 11. In a statement that was printed in the Arabic press but not in the U.S. press, those thinkers—including luminaries from the world of Islamic fundamentalism like the Egyptian Muslim Brothers—expressed their "deep sorrow and sadness," and denounced "firmly and strongly" the attacks that run contrary to all "Islamic and humanitarian values."[78] They then followed up with another statement warning against a war that would harm the people of Afghanistan and called on the international community to work for international justice for the eradication of terrorism.[79] The second statement was also ignored, and the U.S. went ahead with its war of revenge that has as of yet failed to produce bin Laden or to diminish terrorism in any meaningful way.

The United States has been under sustained criticism from Europe and elsewhere for its disregard of international law. Recent administrations have deviated from international consensus on a number of issues, and the Bush administration made it very clear that they did not feel obliged to adhere to the ABM treaty, among other treaties that they are not keen about. The Bush administration could have easily obtained international support for the punishment of the terrorist perpetrators and their patrons. They could have given diplomacy a chance; the Taliban government requested evidence of bin Laden's involvement, and it should have received it. The Taliban government desired negotiations with the U.S., and negotiations could have resulted in the surrender of bin Laden, or his expulsion out of Afghanistan. But the U.S. wanted a war, a clear bombing campaign that could be played on TV screens through the country. The Mufti of al-Azhar University in Cairo, who juridically is perhaps the highest legal authority in Islam, strongly condemned the terrorist act of September 11. He also made it very clear that the submission of evidence is important before proceeding in the punishment. He also added that he opposed any act that results in the death of innocent people.[80] But then again; was it not naïve to expect the U.S. to reverse its historical course and to suddenly and abruptly begin to show consistency and respect for international law in its foreign policy pursuits?

Anti-Americanism will grow. Scenes of U.S. bombings are widely shown on Middle East TV, and only the U.S. public seems to be undisturbed by such scenes. In Europe, the anti-war movement is gaining momentum, even within the ranks of the Labour Party itself in the UK.

One writer sympathetic to the Muslim Brothers in Egypt may have been expressing the sentiments of many angry Arabs and Muslims when he wrote in *Afaq `Arabiyyah* the following poem: "Ye, Oppressors on earth go slow, the sky and the earth have a mighty one; fear God, as one day your injustice may cause you to burn in fire; I have not stolen loans from a bank, and have not embezzled; I have not pursued Terrorism as my course or my religion, not even in thought or dialogue; so why do I become a prisoner, and why do I suffer from chains and gates…?"[81] The U.S. may soon wonder whether there could have been a wiser and more prudent response to the September 11 attacks. It may find that its military war cannot eradicate the desperate conditions which spawn terrorism; very likely, its war will only serve to produce more violence, on all sides. It was easy for the U.S. to initiate its "new war," but it will not be easy to stop; we may come to find that this is a war without end and without conclusions.

NOTES

1 See Gitlin's "Blaming America First," *Mother Jones* (Jan.–Feb. 2002).

2 He caused an uproar in the Muslim world by asserting the superiority of Western civilization and the inferiority of the Islamic civilization. "Italy's Premier Calls Western Civilization Superior to Islamic World," *The New York Times*, September 27, 2001.

3 Huntington, Samuel, *The Clash of Civilization and the Remaking of the World Order* (New York: Simon and Schuster, 1996).

4 This was according to the suggestion of the chief Department of State propagandist (or PR expert, to use the preferred language for U.S. information campaigns) Charlotte Beers. See "She lands the Propaganda Account," *The Los Angeles Times*, November 1, 2001. Beers previously helped Uncle Ben's market its rice.

5 See Carter, Jimmy, *The Blood of Abraham* (Boston: Houghton Mifflin, 1985).

6 Kurtz, Howard, *The Washington Post*, October 31.

7 See Fouad Ajami's op-ed piece in the *New York Times* by the title "For more Benign Neglect in the Mideast," April 14, 1985.

8 See Patai, Raphel, *The Arab Mind* (New York: Schocken, 1973). The books is still used on U.S. college campuses despite being discredited by Middle East academics.

9 Pryce, Jones, David, *The Closed Circle : An Interpretation of the Arabs* (New York: Harper and Row, 1989).

10 Will, George, "Afghans willing to change," *Chicago Sun-Times*, October 26, 2001.

11 See Lewis's "Did you say 'American imperialism'?" *National Review* (Dec. 17, 2001).

12 Lewis, Bernard, *Islam and the West* (New York: Oxford University Press, 1993). This book has gone into numerous editions since at least 1950s.

13 Rodinson, Maxime, *La fascination de l'Islam*,(Paris: ed. la Decouverte, 1989).

14 See *The Economist*, "Islam and the West," November, 17, p. 10.

15 See Bob Woodward's series of articles on the aftermath of September 11 in the *Washington Post* beginning January 27, 2002.

16 Lewis, Bernard, *The Political Language of Islam* (Chicago: University of Chicago Press, 1988).

17 The Muslim Brotherhood is the first modern Islamic political movement which was founded in Egypt by Hasan al-Banna in 1928 in al-Isma`iliyyah. The Brotherhood sought to found a modern political party but with Islam as its ideological foundation. It aspired to apply Islamic laws in society and government, and to resist the penetration of Western laws in Muslim lands. The classic account of the early phase of the movement is Ishaq Musa al-Husayni, *The Muslim Brethren* (Beirut: Khayat, 1956). The movement later inspired the more militant and more radical offshoots that would carry its mantle in more than one Muslim country.

18 See in this regard, Norman, Daniel, *Islam and the West: The Making of an Image* (Edinburgh: Edinburgh University Press, 1960).

19 See Hamady, Sania, *Temperament and Character of the Arabs* (New York: Taywane, 1960).

20 Pipes was appointed to a Defense Department task force in November 2001.

21 Emerson was hired by NBC News as it special expert on terrorism. He was the one who asserted that the Oklahoma City bombing was the work of Islamist terrorists. See the feature on him in *Washington Post*, November 14. The article mysteriously fails to mention his Oklahoma City bombing speculation.

22 Ajami has been for years the CBS News expert on the Middle East.

23 Fandy was friendly with Saudi opposition, before he became an advocate of U.S. foreign policy establishment views. See his "To Reach Arabs, Try Changing the Channel," *Washington Post*, December 21, 2001, which borrows freely from Ajami's piece in *The New York Times Magazine* (see Note 76).

24 See the *Los Angeles Times*, January 11, 2002.

25 All translations from the Koran are the author's.

26 *Sahih Muslim*, Hadith 4623.

27 Shams ad-Din, Muhammad Mahdi, *Fiqh al-`Unf al-Musallah Fi al-Islam* (*The Jurisprudence of Armed Violence in Islam*) (Beirut: al-Mu'assassah ad-Duwaliyyah, 2001).

28 The introduction of the book was published in *al-Hayat*, October 1, p. 10.

29 See his "Dear Saudi Arabia," *New York Times* (December 12, 2001).

30 Wilson, Evan M., *Decision on Palestine: How the U.S. Came to Recognize Israel* (Stanford: Hoover Institution Press, 1979).

31 Nutting, Anthony, *No End of a Lesson: The Story of Suez* (London: Constable, 1967).

32 There are interesting insights and information in this regard in Hersh, Seymour, *The Samson Option: Israel Nuclear Arsenal and American Foreign Policy* (New York: Random House, 1991).

33 See the classic account in Quandt, William, *Peace Process: American Diplomacy and the Arab-Israeli Conflict since 1967* (Berkeley: University of California Press, 1993).

34 Quandt in Peace Process believes it was more responsible in the Egyptian front than the Syrian front.

35 Yergin, Daniel, *The Prize: The Epic Quest for Oil, Money and Power* (New York: Simon and Schuster, 1991).

36 Roosevelt, Archibald, *For Lust of Knowing: Memoirs of An Intelligence Officer* (New York: Little, Brown, 1988).

37 For a penetrating and early critique of the Oslo process, see Said, Edward W., *Peace and Its Discontents* (New York: Vintage, 1995).

38 Agha, Hussein, and Malley, Robert, "Camp David: the Tragedy of Errors," *New York Review of Books*, August 9, 2001.

39 For example, Clinton Middle East "expert" at the National Security Council, a certain Bruce Riedel, asserts that Arab public opinion is not outraged or upset about the suffering of the civilian population in Iraq. See the interview with Riedel in *Middle East Quaterly*, Vol. VI, no. 4 (December 1999).

As`ad AbuKhalil

40 Ibn Battutah, *Rihlat ibn Battutah* (*The Journey of ibn Battutah*), Beirut: Dar Sadir, undated, p. 392.

41 *Mujahideen* is from an Arabic word, and it literally means *perpetrators of jihad*. And if jihad is "holy war," then they are holy warriors. The name was applied in the 1980s to refer to the anti-communist Afghani forces who were fighting the Soviet occupation of their country. They were receiving lavish U.S., Pakistani, and Saudi military and economic aid. Most of the factions were far-right and religious oriented.

42 There are four schools of classical jurisprudence in Sunni Islam: the Shafi`i, the Maliki, Hanafi, and Hanbalite. The Hanbalite is the most conservative and most traditionalist. It has been the most resistant to reform and adaptation.

43 For the crucial influence of `Azzam on bin Laden's life, see one of the earliest books on bin Laden: Naddaf, `Imad, *Osama bin Laden: Wahid Min Milyar* (*Osama bin Laden: One in a Billion*) (Beirut: Mu'assasat al-Iman, 1998), pp. 53-56, 81.

44 On the Algerian Afghans, see the detailed accounts in *al-Hayat*, November 23 and November 24.

45 See the classic account of the rise of the Taliban, Rashid, Ahmed, *Taliban: Militant Islam, Oil and Fundamentalism in Central Asia* (New Haven: Yale University Press, 2000), p. 21.

46 See the interview in *al-Hayat*, January 19 and 20, 2002.

47 See the text of op-ed piece by Zalmay Khalilzad, "Time to Reengage," *The Washington Post*, October 7, 1996.

48 See *The New York Times*, November 25, 2001; and The *Modesto Bee*, November 24, 2001.

49 On this important chapter in Arab contemporary history, see Kerr, Malcolm, *The Arab Cold War* (London: Oxford University Press, 1970).

50 In interviews on al-Jazeera TV in 2000, Prince Talal talked about this period, but claimed without any evidence that he was manipulated by the Egyptian government at the time.

51 For the war of *fatwas* between bin Laden and bin Baz, see *Ruz al-Yusuf*, February 6, 1995.

52 See anonymous, *Ilayki Ukhti al-Muslimah: al-Hijab ash-Shari`i* (*To You My Muslim Sister: The Shar`i Veil*), unplaced and undated.

53 For a succinct overview of the ideas of `Abdul-Wahhab, see Dallal, Ahmad, "The Origins and Objectives of Islamic Revivalist Thought, 1750–1850," in *Journal of the American Oriental Society*, Vol. 113, no. 3 (1993)

54 See Dallal, Ahmad, op. cit., p. 349.

55 See al-Wardani, Salih, *Bin Baz: Faqih al-Saud* (*Bin Baz: The Cleric of the House of Saud*) (Cairo: Dar al-Husam, 1998), p. 102.

56 Bin Baz, `Abdul-`Aziz, *al-Jawab al-Mufid fi Hukm at-Taswir* (*The Useful Answer in the Matter of Photography*) (Jidda: Dar al-Mujtama`, 1987), p. 4.

57 Ibid, p. 45.

58 Ibid, p. 48.

59 See Woodward, Bob, *Veil* (New York: Simon and Schuster, 1987).

60 The narrative of U.S.-Iranian relations is told in James, Bill, *The Eagle and the Lion* (New Haven: Yale University Press, 1988). He has interesting information on the lavish gifts that prominent U.S. journalists used to receive from the Shah. This may explain the fawning coverage of this Iranian dictator in the U.S. press, unlike the European press.

61 The date is listed by the London-based Islamic Information Monitor, which has been linked in the media to bin Laden. See the biography of bin Laden, largely derived from the Monitor sources, in *al-Hayat*, October 4, 2001.

62 Ibid.

63 Ibid.

64 Qutb, Sayyid, *Ma`alim fi at-Tariq* (Signposts on the Road) (Cairo: Dar al-Shuruq, 1997).

65 Al-Zawahiri mentions the role of Qutb in his recently smuggled autobiography, serialized in *ash-Sharq al-Awsat* newspaper in December 2001, under the title *Fursan Tahta Rayat an-Nabi* (*Knights Under the Banner of the Prophet*).

66 See the account of `Abdullah Anas, a comrade of Shah Masoud, in *al-Hayat*, October 30, 2001.

67 Woodward, Bob, *The Commanders* (New York: Simon and Schuster, 1991).

68 Mylroie, Laurie, *Study of Revenge: The First World Trade Center Attack and Saddam Hussein's War Against America* (Washington, DC: AEI Press, 2001).

69 Even the otherwise excellent account by Rashid maintains that. See his *Taliban*, op. cit., p. 136.

70 Abu Qatada appeared on the al-Jazeera's TV program's Akthar Min Ra'y, November 24, 2001. Press reports identified Abu Qatada as a spokesperson, and he certainly speaks as one. Recently the U.K. press identified Abu Qatada (who mysteriously vanished) as an undercover government informer.

71 al-Jazeera is an international news Arabic channel which began broadcasting in October 1996. It is quasi independent but receives subsidies from the Qatari government. It is available to some 150 thousands Dish Network subscribers in the U.S., and to more than 35 million viewers in the Arab world.

72 Israel is a democracy for its Jewish citizens, while there is enough literature on the pattern of Israeli discrimination against Arab citizens of the state. See Smooha, Sami, *Israel: Pluralism and Conflict* (Berkeley: University of California Press, 1978) and Jiryis, Sabri, *The Arabs in Israel* (New York: Monthly Review Press, 1976).

73 The full text is reprinted in Qubaysi, Muhammad, and ad-Darwish, `Adnan, *Bin Laden `Ala Difaf Bahr Qazwin [Bin Laden on the Shores of the Caspian Sea]*, Beirut: 2001, p. 289.

74 See Fisk, Robert, *Pity the Nation: Lebanon at War* (London: Oxford University Press, 1991).

75 See Tamman, Maurice, "Tracing the money: 27 groups, individuals on target list," *Atlanta Journal and Constitution*, September 25, 2001, p. 11A.

76 Of course, the U.S. government was bothered by this independent news source especially that it airs strong criticisms of U.S. and Israeli policies and actions in the region. Right-wing Middle East expert Fouad Ajami distorts the contents of the channel to dis-

credit it. See his "What the Muslim World is Watching," *New York Times Magazine*, November 18, 2001.

77 See the article by Bob Woodward and Dan Balz, *Washington Post*, January 27, 2002.

78 The full text was printed in *al-Quds al-`Arabi*, September 14, 2001.

79 See *al-Quds al-`Arabi*, September 24, 2001.

80 See the statement of Shaykh al-Azhar in Qubaysi, Muhammad, and ad-Darwish, `Adnan, op. cit., pp. 191-192.

81 This was published in *Afaq `Arabiyyah*, November 21, 2001.

As`ad AbuKhalil

BIBLIOGRAPHY

AbuKhalil, As`ad, "Against the Taboos of Islam:Anti-Conformist Trends in Contemporary Arab Islamic Thought," in W. Zartman and Charles Butterworth, eds., *Between State and Islam* (New York: Cambridge University Press, 2000).

———, "The Incoherence of Islamic Fundamentalists: Arab Islamic Thought at the End of the 20th Century," *The Middle East Journal,* Autumn 1994.

Chomsky, Noam, *The Fateful Triangle* (Boston, South End Press, 1983).

Cooley, John, *Payback: America's Long War in the Middle East* (Riverside, NJ: Macmillan, 1991).

———, *Unholy Wars: Afghanisan, America and International Terrorism* (Sterling, VA: Pluto Press, 1999).

Dallal, Ahmad, "The Origins and Objectives of Islamic Revivalist Thought, 1750-1850," in *Journal of the American Oriental Society,* Vol. 113, No. 3 (1993).Halliday, Fred, *Arabia Without Sultans* (New York: Penguin, 1974).

Djait, Hichem, *L'Europe et l'Islam* (Paris: Seuil, 1978).

Esposito, John, *Islam and Politics* (Syracuse: Syracuse University Press, 1998).

Hourani, Albert, *Islam in European Thought* (New York: Cambridge University Press, 1991).

Hudson, Michael, *Arab Politics: The Search for Legitimacy* (New Haven: Yale University Press, 1977).

James, Bill, *The Eagle and the Lion* (New Haven: Yale University Press, 1988).

Kepel, Gilles, *Les Banlieues de l'Islam* (Paris: Seuil, 1987).

Khalidi, Rashid, *Palestinian Identity: The Construction of Modern National Consciousness* (New York: Columbia University Press, 1997).

Khalidi, Walid, ed., *From Haven to Conquest* (Beirut: Institute for Palestine Studies, 1971).

Mas`ad, Joseph, "Palestinians and the Limits of Racialized Discourse," in *Social Text*, No. 34, 1993.

———, "On Zionism and Jewish Supremacy," in *New Politics*, Spring 2002.

Rashid, Ahmed, *Taliban: Militant Islam, Oil, and Fundamentalism in Central Asia* (New Haven: Yale University Press, 2000).

Rodinson, Maxime, *La Fascination de l'Islam* (Paris: La Decouverte, 1989).

Roy, Olivier, *La Guerre d'Afghanistan: intervention sovietique at resistance* (Paris: La Documentation Francaise, 1985).

Said, Edward, *Orientalism* (New York: Pantheon, 1978).

———, *Covering Islam* (New York: Pantheon, 1981).

Schimmel, Annemarie, *Islam* (Albany, New York: SUNY Press, 1982).

Smith, Charles D., *Palestine and the Arab Israeli Conflict* (New York: St. Martin's, 1994).

As`ad AbuKhalil

ABOUT THE AUTHOR

AS'AD ABUKHALIL was born in Tyre, Lebanon. He received his B.A. and M.A. in Political Science from the American University of Beirut, and his Ph.D. in Comparative Politics from Georgetown University. AbuKhalil has taught at Georgetown, George Washington University, Tufts University, Colorado College, and Randolph-Macon Woman's College. He was a Scholar-in-Residence at the Middle East Institute in Washington, D.C., in 1992. He is the author of *Historical Dictionary of Lebanon* (1988). His articles on Middle East politics and society have appeared in English, German, Spanish, and Arabic. He is associate professor of political science at California State University, Stanislaus, and Research Fellow at the Center for Middle Eastern Studies at the University of California at Berkeley.

OTHER OPEN MEDIA BOOKS

9-11
Noam Chomsky
128 pages / $8.95 / ISBN: 1-58322-489-0

TERRORISM AND WAR
Howard Zinn
160 pages / $9.95 / ISBN: 1-58322-493-9

THE OPEN MEDIA PAMPHLET SERIES

CORPORATE MEDIA
AND THE THREAT TO DEMOCRACY
Robert W. McChesney
80 pages / $5.95 / ISBN: 1-888363-47-9

MEDIA CONTROL
The Spectacular Achievements of Propaganda
Noam Chomsky
64 pages / $5.95 / ISBN: 1-888363-49-5

GENE WARS
The Politics of Biotechnology
Kristin Dawkins
64 pages / $4.95 / ISBN: 1-888363-48-7

GLOBALIZING CIVIL SOCIETY
Reclaiming Our Right to Power
David C. Korten
80 pages / $5.95 / ISBN: 1-888363-59-2

ZAPATISTA ENCUENTRO
Documents from the 1996 Encounter for
Humanity Against Neoliberalism
The Zapatistas
64 pages / $5.95 / ISBN: 1-888363-58-4

IT'S THE MEDIA, STUPID
John Nichols and Robert W. McChesney
128 pages / $10.00 / ISBN: 1-58322-029-1

CUTTING CORPORATE WELFARE
Ralph Nader
144 pages / $10.00 / ISBN: 1-58322-033-X

THE WTO
Five Years of Reasons to Resist
Corporate Globalization
Lori Wallach and Michelle Sforza
Introduction by Ralph Nader
80 pages / $5.95 / ISBN: 1-58322-035-6

THE CASE OF MUMIA ABU-JAMAL
A Life in the Balance
Amnesty International
64 pages / $6.95 / ISBN: 1-58322-081-X

ISLANDS OF RESISTANCE
Puerto Rico, Vieques, and U.S. Policy
Mario Murillo
96 pages / $6.95 / ISBN: 1-58322-080-1

WEAPONS IN SPACE
Karl Grossman
96 pages / $6.95 / ISBN: 1-58322-044-5

10 REASONS TO ABOLISH THE IMF & WORLD BANK
Kevin Dahaner
104 pages / $6.95 / ISBN: 1-58322-464-5

SENT BY EARTH
Alice Walker
64 pages / $5.00 / ISBN: 1-58322-491-2

TERRORISM: THEIRS AND OURS
Eqbal Ahmad
64 pages / $6.95 / ISBN: 1-58322-490-4